Picturing people

British figurative art since 1945

The British Council

The British Council

The British Council promotes cultural, educational and technical co-operation between Britain and other countries. Its work develops world-wide partnerships and improves international understanding.

The Council is represented in 87 countries, where it runs 143 offices, 116 libraries and 52 English teaching centres. The Council provides an unrivalled network of contacts with government departments, universities, embassies, professional bodies, and business and industry in Britain and overseas.

The Council's annual turnover is £312 million, including government grants and overseas aid programmes. Its own earnings now exceed £68 million.

The British Council is an independent, non-political organization.

All enquiries on content to Visual Arts Department, The British Council.

Published by The British Council, 10 Spring Gardens, London SW1A 2BN

ISBN 0 86355 089 4

Cover: detail from Eileen Cooper's *Gift*, 1985 [No. 23]

Selector and author: Norbert Lynton
Exhibition Officer: Ann Elliott
Exhibition Assistant: Nicola Coleby

Design: The British Council
Typesetting: OTS (Typesetting) Ltd, Caterham, Surrey

Printed in Hong Kong by Graphic Directions, Des Voeux Road, Central Hong Kong

Picturing people

British figurative art since 1945

Kuala Lumpur, National Art Gallery
2 – 31 December 1989

Hong Kong Museum of Art
19 January – 25 March 1990

Singapore, The Empress Place
20 April – 5 May 1990

Acknowledgements

In addition to all of the artists, lenders to the
exhibition anonymous and listed in the catalogue,
and the staff of the art galleries participating in the
exhibition's tour, the organizers would like to thank:

Gillian Adam
Judy Adam
Lucy Aspinall
Kate Austin
Anne Barlow
V Beston
Philip Blackman
Ruth Bubb
Elizabeth Cardosa
Rita Charles
Honor Clerk
Jill Constantine
Vivian Dacre
Kate Deasington
Neil Denman
John Erle Drax
Matthew Flowers
Robin Gibson
Mark Glazebrook
Jan Graffius
Pam Griffin
Gill Hedley
Craig Henderson
Rosemary Hood
Isobel Johnstone
Kasmin
Karen Kuhlman
Bing Cheng Liu
Nicola Liu
Gerry Ma
Jamie MacLean
Nigel McKernaghan
MoMart
John Murphy
Fionnuala O'Connell
Isabella Oulton
Elizabeth Payne
Jane Penny
Barbara Putt
John Roberts
Andrea Rose
Peter Rumley
Nigel Semmens
Sarah Shott
Andrew Spells
Lena St George-Sweet
Margaret Thornton
Estella Tong
Muriel Wilson
Paul Woodcock
Kai Kin Yung

Foreword

During the 1980s, in Britain and particularly in Scotland, there has been a resurgence of interest in figurative painting, almost as if it had just been discovered. In fact, artists working in this way had never ceased to paint, but continued out of the limelight which shone in the 1960s and 1970s on the abstract, the minimalist and the conceptual.

We hope that this exhibition will demonstrate the continuum. It is not intended to be an exhaustive survey, since this would be an impossible task within the limit of sixty canvases. Instead, Norbert Lynton has chosen paintings that interact within a predetermined structure, with the intention that this should add to our understanding and enjoyment of some very fine individual works. I am particularly grateful to Professor Lynton, who came to us with the initial proposal for this exhibition, and who has given unsparingly of his time and efforts over the past year, as has my colleague, Ann Elliott, who has worked with him in all the preparations, assisted by Nicola Coleby.

None of this would be possible without the collaboration of the artists, their galleries and those individuals and institutions whose works form this collection. I thank them all for their great generosity. Finally I should like to express my heartfelt thanks to the three galleries in the Far East and our British Council colleagues in those countries, together with whom we take pleasure in presenting this exhibition.

Henry Meyric Hughes
Director Visual Arts Department
The British Council

Contents

Norbert Lynton

Norbert Lynton, born in 1927, is an art historian and writer, specializing in contemporary art. He began his career by lecturing in art history at Leeds College of Art and then at Chelsea School of Art in London. From 1965 to 1970 he was art critic for the *Guardian* newspaper and for the next five years was Director of exhibitions for the Arts Council of Great Britain. From 1975 to 1988 Norbert Lynton was Professor of History of Art at the University of Sussex, and for the last three years, before his retirement in 1988, he was Dean of the School of European Studies. He has published many articles, art catalogues and books, notably *The Story of Modern Art*, a revised version of which was published by Phaidon in 1989.

Introduction

We all tend to speak of art in terms of selected individuals or prominent movements. Neither focus conveys anything like the truth. We tell our story selectively because we want to keep it clear and also to show our preferences, and thus we falsify it. Art is many things, and it is the coexistence of diverse sorts of art, produced by artists young and not young, new and familiar, that lies at the heart of the tale.

In British art the last forty-five years have been amazingly lively and productive. This is perhaps equally true of British music, writing, theatre and film-making. But in the visual arts it is especially surprising since the previous hundred years, though full of interest and important adventures, had suggested that Britain would never be better than a secondary artistic force. In the nineteenth century and until the 1930s, Paris was the centre of Western art. In the post-war years the focus shifted to the United States, especially to New York: the New American Painting, as it was called, was developed there to prove the emancipation of American art from European masters and methods. Its impact on Western art was immense in the later 1950s and 1960s, suggesting that the most powerful Western country politically and economically was also the leader in Western, if not global art. New York thus took over from Paris – but this of course also implied that nowhere would be art's Mecca for always. Today, though new art thrives in the United States and is promoted and received there with an avidity artists elsewhere cannot but envy, we hear of it and meet it rarely in Europe. The American dominance has ended.

Time will show whether that dominance was productive. In Britain the coming of, especially, American Abstract Expressionism was a great energizing event. Many British artists responded to it positively; those who could, visited New York to make closer contact. After overcoming what now seems a surprisingly dense prejudice against this art, British critics switched to welcoming it as a kind of renaissance – a new set of priorities, a new set of values. These conflicted with those indigenous to Britain, most obviously a preference for lyrical art, a visual poetry to do with landscape's spaces, atmosphere and mobility. The St Ives School provided the avant-garde in the 1950s. Ben Nicholson, who had created something close to pure, Constructivist abstraction in the 1930s, now moved freely between abstraction and semi-representational art, frequently on still-life themes. Younger painters of the School, notably Patrick Heron and Roger Hilton, had wedded Paris-inspired pictorial devices to their apprehension of landscape. Abstract Expressionism now gave absolute priority to abstract form and colour and insisted on art as a mirroring of deep, preferably unconscious motivation at the expense of external motifs, however much abstracted. The opposition seemed total, yet it is striking that it was precisely painters like Heron and Hilton who responded with admiration to American exhibitions in London and made contact with the major painters in New York.

None the less, there was a marked contrast between America's enormous and often explosively formless canvases and the modest size and usually gentle manners of the St Ives School. In 1960-61 a group of younger British artists exhibited in London under the label Situation, showing mostly very large, wholly abstract and geo-metrically articulated paintings. This almost architectonic art, less openly expressive than the American work it confronted, looked alien and drew strong criticism. It claimed for itself an international rather than a British or, least of all, English position. It would still look alien today, yet it profoundly changed our conception of what modern painting could be. One of its messages was that there was an alternative both to the English attachment to landscape formulas and to American subjectivism: a designed art, of clear forms displayed on a large surface, without gesture though still with individual character. The Op art tendency that emerged soon after owed much to this confirmation, as well as to the Constructivist tradition that had come out of revolutionary Russia.

Pop art emerged in 1961-62, the product of a number of senior painting students, mostly in London's art schools. Its images were narrative, at times polemical, frequently jokey, but above all figurative. The British media leapt with relief at this new movement. It made news, it was cheeky, it was young, it was self-evidently British. Its roots were not in English landscape painting but in the tradition of narrative art initiated by Hogarth in the eighteenth century and developed into a broad stream in the nineteenth century until Modernism seemed to veto it. Now art was fun again, and when it was not fun it was accessible as image and content. The best Pop and Op painters were welcomed in Western Europe and in America with an interest no previous British movement had attracted in this century. What is more, British Pop art was seen as an essentially British creation, parallel to but also wholly distinct from the American Pop movement.

All this meant public notice, public activity (exhibi-tions, publications, television programmes). There was even an expectation of broad popularity for Pop art since it was readily associated with pop music, with lively new ideas in fashion and other design areas, and with the whole youth-led ferment that was labelled 'swinging London'. The new art movements enhanced the image of art as a career at a time when the art schools were being strengthened and enlarged, but then also blocked the path into the commercial system for the younger artists, who in many cases were taught by the movements' leaders. By the late 1960s a counter tendency was emerging. Its existence was not properly acknowledged in Britain until 1972 and the exhibition *The New Art* (held at the Hayward Gallery in London), but its initiators had already been noticed in other European countries. Conceptualism, as it became known, challenged the assumptions forming the modern view of art and appeared to attack the commercial and museum system. Most of all, it questioned the need for an object as a necessary embodiment of the artist's work. It proposed ideas and polemical positions, and delivered these through words or images or enactments (including live performance) that were certainly not paintings or sculptures or other recognized art objects. It was not, as was said, wholly intellectual and devoid of emotional force; it did not in fact remove all aesthetic interest from art production; it was not necessarily difficult though the charge of obscurantism was laid against it – but it certainly contrasted sharply with what until recently had been the new art, especially with Abstract Expressionism's emotional display and the youthful jollity of much of Pop art. Conceptual art still flourishes, and it should be noted that it eludes the abstract/figurative barrier that has long worked against the deeper understanding of modern art.

The 1980s saw the return of figurative art. It had of course never ceased to exist – Pop art had been essentially figurative painting – yet the critics' cry was suddenly that figurative art had been reborn, or at least released, after repression by Conceptualism and other avant-garde tendencies. There was certainly a new emphasis on figurative painting, to some extent led by their claims, and some of this showed qualities that were both new and innovatingly traditional. Much of the new work was emphatically painterly: full-blooded, expressive, rich. It was also communicative, using narrative and/or symbolism and a wealth of effective pictorial devices. The critics' campaign worked well. New figurative painters received notice and bred others. Older figurative painters, long undervalued, were now presented as significant masters. Purchasers came forward, perhaps because of easier financial circumstances at some levels of British society, partly because of a new image of the business executive as someone in touch with new art as well as design, but mostly because this new art was relatively accessible to a wide public. Certain Continental tendencies, especially in Germany, seemed to be in sympathy with it and had some influence on it:

America's ascendancy in art suddenly faded. Some of the new names on the British art scene came not as in the past from London or the south of England, but from art schools outside London, most notably in Glasgow. The Glasgow School of Art is now associated with a markedly energetic group of figurative painters, working in a variety of styles but generally with vehemence and with social point.

This summary of developments in British art since 1945 has ignored the activity of important individual artists, with or without group affiliations. Recently there has been an attempt to corral some of them under a new label, the School of London. It was proposed by the painter R B Kitaj in a catalogue text of 1976 and has been picked up by others since then and broadened in the process. The intention was not to identify the capital city with a particular tendency but rather to suggest that among London's many artists there were some sharing certain priorities. It becomes ever harder to say what these priorities are. Kitaj associated his fictive group with his own emphasis on drawing and painting the naked and the clothed figure from observation, in the tradition of French nineteenth-century practice and especially of Degas. The term has been stretched to accommodate a variety of other figurative painters, notably Francis Bacon, our internationally most renowned figurative painter, together with David Hockney, Frank Auerbach and Ken Kiff. Yet William Coldstream's and Euan Uglow's patient transcriptions of a deliberately posed model do not seem to qualify them for the School, and I am not sure why: they are thought of as calculating painters, more intent on an optically exact and geometrically satisfying mapping of all the key points in a composition than on the dialogue between the human motif and the artist. I see them as engaged in a passionate dialogue which honours the human being as much as it does the perplexities of representing a living being and its setting via marks on a canvas.

A long list could be made of the figurative painters working in Britain in these years, now deemed to be the pioneers of the new figurative art. Stanley Spencer rightly holds the place of honour, working directly from the human material around him and from the faith implanted in him in childhood. He was distinct from any art movement yet is central to a longer view of English art with its love of story-telling, its realism modified by linearity and humour, and its partly unconscious inclination to religious themes. The young David Hockney is known to have admired Spencer; so did his professor of painting at the Royal College of Art, Carel Weight. At present, Spencer still tends to be seen as an eccentric, as though his unconventional and sometimes offensive social behaviour defined his work. There are several other names that should be mentioned, among them Francis Bacon, Richard Hamilton, Frank Auerbach, Ken Kiff, Leon Kossoff, Lucian Freud. They are distinct and could be said to share only the most general of aims, but there is a sense in which their coexistence stimulates them and it is in this real but vague sense that there may indeed be something like a School of London.

Most of the individual characteristics we can find in the younger painters' figurative work can be traced to one or other of these artists and to impulses from German and other Continental painters. Yet recent figurative art also has its own qualities. I have spoken already of its fullness; it shows also a desire to communicate, through narrative, myth, quotations and other devices. Much of it is openly autobiographical; some of it teases us with clever references; occasionally it indulges in juggling with, or confounding, outdated pictorial idioms. Much of it is grave in tone and some of it is openly polemical in the area of politics and social well-being. There can be no doubt that some major new talents have emerged within this rapidly promoted new wave, and no doubt that they will develop their work and prove their staying power in the future. At the same time, there is evidence that other young artists are again finding the comparatively unsung virtues of abstract painting as challenging and appealing as those of figuration, drawn perhaps by its relative silence amid the near-hubbub of current figurative art.

The broad selection of work offered in this exhibition thus reflects only part of recent and contemporary British art production. Our interpretation of the term 'figurative' is an all-embracing one. It is sometimes used to mean representational as opposed to abstract: here it indicates priority given to the human image whether or not it is taken from observation. Our list of exhibiting artists does not adhere to any evident agreed national register. It includes many of the most admired figurative painters of the present and recent past, as well as featuring some less well-known painters, present here not only because of their interest and quality but also to suggest the wide diversity of what is being done.

The invitation offered by this exhibition is thus not the usual one of 'Come and admire the work of these more or less famous artists'. Too many exhibitions, I believe, are or seem to be about art alone. We do not read books just to know about books; we do not listen to music just to be able to say to ourselves that we have listened to the work of this composer, or that performer. We do these things in order to deepen our understanding of ourselves and of our fellow beings through the words and sounds given us by others. The same is of course true of what artists set before us, yet we have tended to disregard this essential function in modern times. Hence the variety of work in the exhibition. Comparisons and contrasts bring out art's artificiality and thus also its insistence on meaning and purpose. Hence also, where apposite, the stress on the content of each exhibit in the pages that follow – content both as iconography and as manner. The colour or space or formal organization of an image addresses us directly, but then so does an image that we identify and enter into an imaginative relationship with. I hope that visitors to this exhibition will find that, while their knowledge of particular works by particular artists working in a particular country has been enhanced, so too has their intimacy with art and thus their sense of art's power and purposes.

Norbert Lynton

Portraits and personalities

Craigie Aitchison
William Bowyer
Paul Brason
Jeffery Camp
William Coldstream
Patrick George
Maggi Hambling
David Hockney
Rodrigo Moynihan
Humphrey Ocean
Bryan Organ
Ruskin Spear
Stanley Spencer
Graham Sutherland
David Tindle
Euan Uglow

Portraits and personalities

The three sections into which this exhibition is divided
are not discrete. In using them, we want to suggest that the
many purposes of art – of figurative painting on this
occasion – result in alternative forms and methods. Portrait
painting has a long tradition in the West. According to
Greek legend, painting and drawing first began when a
young woman drew a line around the shadow of her lover
before his departure. What the Greeks left to posterity,
however, was not private, informal portraits but representations of gods and heroes, public images. The private,
informal portrait became a normal form of art much later,
around 1500.

We expect a portrait to be lifelike, or to give the
impression of being lifelike, and that has been one of the
criteria determining what could go into this category. We
may also want a portrait to inform us about the sitter. In
fact, many portraits tell us little or nothing. Some sitters we
are likely to recognize: Dame Peggy Ashcroft and Dirk
Bogarde, both admired actors [Nos.11 and 17], and perhaps
Viv Richards, the charismatic cricketer [No.2]. Others are
private. Aitchison, Camp, George and Uglow painted their
portraits [Nos.1, 4, 6 and 18] for reasons of affection and
artistic interest; it does not matter that we do not know the
sitters. What does matter is whether their paintings can
deliver to us a sense of presence and of value. The most
informative portraits here are those of Brason, Hambling
and Spear. They demonstrate different ways of adding
information to likeness. Spear's great civil servant wears the
uniform of his profession but does not reveal his standing
within it [No.14]. The two great women scientists painted by
Hambling and by Spencer [Nos.7 and 15] are portrayed with
and without the accessories that point to their work.
Ocean's bishop [No.12] carries his staff of office and stands
outside his primary cathedral. There are direct symbolical
references here, as there are indirect ones in Hockney's
photographic portrait of his mother [No.8]. For a portrait, or
any other picture, to have value as art it must also bear the
stamp of the artist's conception of what art is. A portrait is
not a reproduction of the sitter but a statement about him or
her and about art as such.

Craigie Aitchison
Portrait of Bruce Marcus

Aitchinson's images are always highly concentrated.
Form and space are radically simplified and the fullest
expression is given to a few resonant colours. His subjects
are often directly religious, but even when they are not
there is a pious, devotional quality to his paintings as
though the act of painting was for him also an act of
reverence and thanksgiving. Note the refinements within
what strikes one first as a very simple thing: the delicacy of
the entire surface composed of subtle washes of oil paint
and quite without the plasticity that others exploit in using
oils; the flatness of the image counteracted by gentle but
crucial changes of tone within colour areas, as in the face
and the T-shirt. Very telling also are the fine, sharp details
and edges that come with the broad colour areas, and the
thin line of light that comes between adjacent colour areas
and helps the portrait to glow. Above all there is the colour
itself: the surprising, luminous red setting of the relatively
dark colours of the man's head and shoulders. By means of
something close to magic Aitchison achieves a tremendous
sense of physical presence although he seems to be playing
down the physical quality of his sitter as also of his paints.
At the same time there is a stillness about the whole picture
that gives it extra force, imprinting it on our memories as an
image of great dignity and significance. Other painters'
portraits tend to seem garrulous in contrast, even, for
example, David Tindle's of Dirk Bogarde [No.17], although
that, too, concentrates on the sitter with value-conferring
intensity.

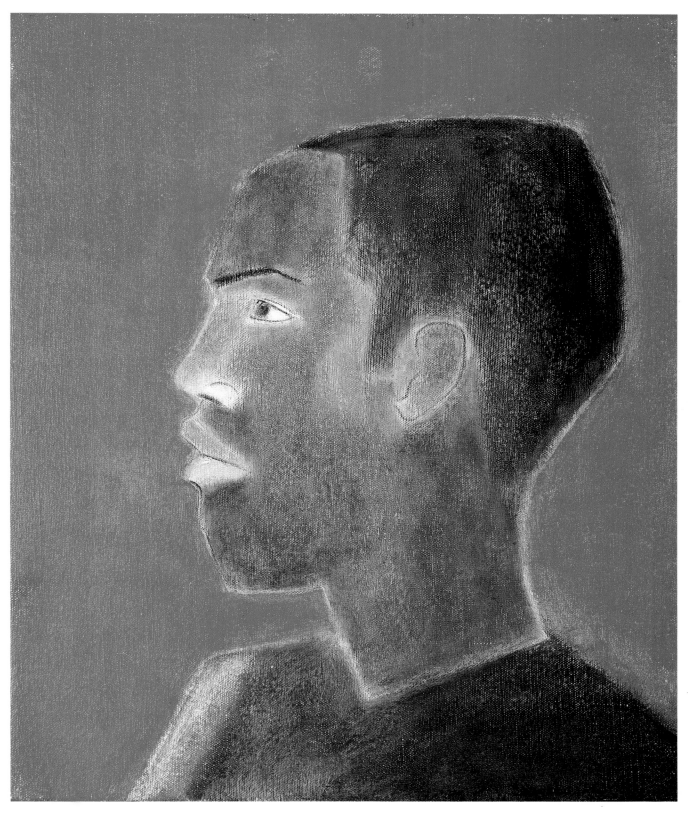

No. 1
Portrait of Bruce Marcus
1986 – 87, oil on canvas
30.5 x 25.4 cm
private collection
photograph: Albemarle Gallery

William Bowyer
Isaac Vivian Alexander ('Viv') Richards

Roman copy after Discobolus by Myro courtesy of Hirmer Fotoarchiv, Munich

A very great batsman, certainly one of the most admired personalities in the international world of cricket, Viv Richards was born in Antigua, in the West Indies, in 1952. He began to play first-class cricket twenty years later and was soon playing for the cricket team of the county of Somerset in England. He is now a member of the Glamorgan team and also captains the West Indies team, probably the best in the world. In 1976 he set a new record when he scored an aggregate of 1,710 runs, with an average score of 90 runs per innings. The National Portrait Gallery recognized his importance and also his popularity in commissioning this portrait.

Richards is defending a wicket; as he hits the ball his head turns to watch its progress to the boundary. He is in focus. The other player, moving as the ball is bowled, seems almost transparent. The crowd is quite unfocused: we get a sensation of the presence of people, not a detailed account. All this, together with the low viewpoint, gives the batsman a heroic image. A photograph provided the basis for the painting but translating it into a convincing painted image required skill and boldness. Consciously or unconsciously, the painter may have been stimulated by a famous sporting image from long ago in the history of Western art: the Greek sculptor Myron's work, done about 2,450 years ago, of a man going through the complex motions called for in throwing a discus. The primary view of the sculpture shows most of the body in profile, the head more or less full face. Richards is shown similarly in the painting.

Bowyer's lively use of paint contributes a great deal to the vividness of the picture, and represents another tradition, that of vigorous, expressive oil painting, developed in sixteenth-century Venice and extended in, especially, the art of Goya.

No. 2
Isaac Vivian Alexander ('Viv') Richards
1986, oil on canvas
93.2 x 76 cm
National Portrait Gallery, London
photograph: National Portrait Gallery

Paul Brason
Sir Roy Strong (Young Man among Roses)

Paul Brason has painted two portraits of Sir Roy Strong, in both of them using Sir Roy's garden as the setting. Roy Strong is an eminent art historian, known especially for his work on Tudor portraiture; he is also an enthusiastic expert on the history of gardening and of cookery. This portrait aptly alludes to a famous example from the history of English painting, housed in the collection of the Victoria and Albert Museum in London of which Sir Roy was director from 1974 to 1987: Nicholas Hilliard's *Young Man among Roses*, a miniature painted four hundred years ago, less than fourteen centimetres high.

That young man is thought to be the second Earl of Essex, known as the unhappy platonic lover of his queen, Elizabeth I. He stands among roses, symbolizing the passion of love, and englantine, a flower associated particularly with the queen. We need not assume that Brason in his picture intended a reference to Queen Elizabeth II in adopting these motifs, nor does his sitter show or simulate love's yearnings. The romance of the old miniature has been sacrificed for clarity and dignity. The roses rest on the seat of a fine seventeenth-century chair on which Sir Roy leans elegantly; the englantine spreads behind him, whereas, in the Hilliard, Essex appears helplessly trapped in a thicket of growing flowers. Brason's detail and manner suggest that his portrait is based on photographs. The result is a convincing representation that also captures some part of the sitter's character where the Hilliard is more generalized, more intent perhaps on showing a fine pair of legs than on guaranteeing something true to life.

Nicholas Hilliard
Young Man among Roses
c.1588, water-based paint
on vellum
by courtesy of the Board
of Trustees of the Victoria
and Albert Museum

No. 3
Sir Roy Strong (Young Man among Roses)
1988, oil on canvas
102 x 71 cm
Gartmore Investment Management Limited
photograph: Gartmore Investment
Management Limited

Jeffery Camp
Chelsea

This frontal portrait suggests both the informative function of the passport photograph and the idealized permanency of a religious icon: in both the face is delineated with little indication of mass. Behind the portrait we see the River Thames and Chelsea Bridge (to which the title refers). There is a particular visual poetry here that seems characteristic of Camp's work. He often combines landscapes or seascapes with foreground figures, making our eyes leap dizzyingly from the near to the far, sometimes implying the frailty of humanity as against nature's persistent powers. Here I think the unstated theme goes further. The frontal head is carefully located in the circle of the painting. The line of the bridge coincides with the sitter's eyes and eyebrows, intense and visionary. The circular format hints at a halo around his head.

The subject is a fellow artist, Neil Jeffries, well known for his deep reliefs – constructed of wood and metal, and painted – which illustrate and comment on aspects of contemporary life with acuity and humour. Camp's delicate, deeply romantic use of colour, tone and line is quite different from the work of his friend. Notice, for example, the spiritualizing effect of those lines of near-white between Jeffries' neck and the blue-grey-green of the river, and the way his hair almost becomes one with the sky behind it.

No. 4
Chelsea
1988, oil on canvas
68 cm diameter
Nigel Greenwood Gallery, London W1
photograph: courtesy Nigel Greenwood
Gallery, London

William Coldstream
Sir John Nicoll

The English have long enjoyed portraits of eminent individuals caught at a relaxed rather than an official, formal moment. Nicoll is seen wearing his uniform and medals, yet here he is off-stage, so to speak, sitting for the painter and detached from his duties as Governor and Commander-in-Chief. In fact, he sat for his portrait in Coldstream's studio at the Slade School of Art in London. Sir John Nicoll was knighted in 1953. He had embarked on a career as a diplomat after studies at Oxford and a period as soldier in 1918-19. He worked for the Foreign Office in Borneo, Tanganyika and Trinidad; then as Colonial Secretary in Fiji and Hong Kong; and finally as Governor of Singapore in 1952-53. The picture was begun in 1953 and completed soon after Nicoll retired.

Coldstream was a man of strong convictions and feelings. He saw art's business as that of recording what was there to be seen, trusting to his eye and to visual measurements which determined the location of the main features of the subject on his canvas. He noted these points by means of little vertical and horizontal strokes; some of these can still be seen but many others have been painted over. Thus, he gradually built up an image true to his optical scanning, a calm, strong record of it and of the space it inhabited. The design of the picture as a whole is carefully judged to support the presence of the subject (figure and chair) and also to convey the sense of air and light. The picture surface, as an aesthetic order with its own satisfactions, is countered by establishing, through that same surface, the living presence, principally via developing face and hands and indicating the body as volume. It would be hard for us to say which of these two functions of the painting had priority. Colour is used aptly but is subsidiary to tone and atmosphere. The sitter's personality is hinted at in the portrait; the painter's is intentionally undeclared – yet I would argue that every part of this careful, undemonstrative work speaks of a quiet, delicate passion, of sensitivity as well as intelligence, of an appetite for new experience and also of a high regard for the traditions of portrait painting.

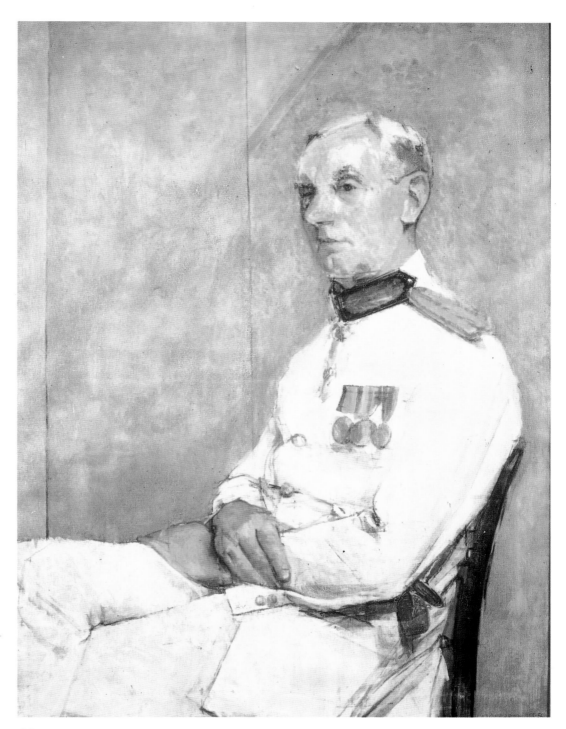

No. 5
Sir John Nicoll
1953 – 56, oil on canvas
106 x 74.9 cm
National Museum's Singapore Collection
photograph: National Museum of Singapore,
courtesy of Dr Peter Rumley

Patrick George
Night Portrait (Hilary Lane)

Night Portrait is the result of several sittings during
which the painter observed and recorded the head and
shoulders of one of his students (at the Slade School of Art
in London) under particular conditions of light. Hilary
Lane, now director of the gallery of the Gardner Centre for
the Arts, University of Sussex, recalls the sheer pain of
sitting still for long periods, and also the almost scientific
care with which the painter, sometimes using a plumb-line,
more often holding the handle of his brush at arm's length
to make measurements and establish visual coordinates,
struggled to 'pin down' (as he put it) his chosen motif. Yet
for all the labour and time it entailed, the painting is
outstandingly fresh and lively. It is of course a personal,
entirely informal work – unlike, for example, the portrait
by George's master, William Coldstream [No.5]. The yellow
patch on the girl's nose is the electric light from an
ordinary domestic bulb hanging in the small room the
painter was using as his London studio.

No. 6
Night Portrait (Hilary Lane)
1965 – 66, oil on canvas
107 x 91.5 cm
the artist
photograph: Rodney Todd-White

Maggi Hambling
Dorothy Hodgkin

Professor Dorothy Hodgkin is one of the country's most eminent scientists, admired especially for her X-ray analysis of vitamin B_{12} (for which she was awarded the Nobel prize in 1964) and the structure of insulin. Maggi Hambling says she found her a most inspiring person and subject.

The painter visited Professor Hodgkin in her Warwickshire home. They met in the garden and then went round the house. Hambling decided that the study had to be the right setting for this portrait; it should show the professor at work, 'making magic'. There was snow on the ground outside, adding to the brilliance of the light coming into the room. There we see the scientist, still hard at work in her seventies, among her books, files and papers. Beside her stands her model of the four molecules of insulin. Her old hands write and hold papers and clutch the magnifying glass. It was not a conscious invention on Hambling's part to show the sitter with two pairs of hands: they happened during the first day of painting and they felt right for the subject. Professor Hodgkin describes herself as an 'experimentalist' among scientists, someone who 'thinks with her hands'.

Hambling was conscious of greatness and also of directness and simplicity. There is perhaps something very English about this portrait: an eminent person, of world renown, at her daily, ordinary tasks at home – at once an understatement and a true account. Anything more formal, more public, would have been a histrionic act, an exaggeration for the sake of effect, and this would not appeal to the Dorothy Hodgkins of this world. Professor Hodgkin was awarded Britain's most distinguished intellectual honour, the Order of Merit, in 1965. Maggi Hambling speaks of her as a woman of exceptional awareness of, and responsiveness to, everything in the world, and one feels that all the information in the painting, all that lightly-carried detail, echoes those qualities. Professor Hodgkin seemed to Hambling an unusually 'enlightened' woman; the accident of snow outside simply added to the illumination in which she works.

No. 9
Philip
1988, oil on canvas
61 x 30.5 cm
courtesy of David Hockney
photograph:
courtesy David Hockney

No. 10
Philip
1988, colour laser print
taken directly from the
oil painting of Philip
169.5 x 115.6 cm
courtesy of David Hockney

Rodrigo Moynihan
Dame Peggy Ashcroft

The National Portrait Gallery commissioned this portrait of one of Britain's most admired actresses at a time when television was crowning her career with wide popularity. Peggy Ashcroft played a secondary part in the television series about India, *The Jewel in the Crown*, giving her role a warmth and weight that made her important to millions of viewers.

She has starred on the British stage for more than half a century, from the time she played Desdemona to Paul Robeson's Othello in 1930. Today there is a fine theatre in Croydon named in her honour. In 1956 she was made a Dame of the British Empire, and in 1985 she won an Oscar in Hollywood for her part in the film *A Passage to India*. She is a retiring, dignified, quietly humorous woman of marked intelligence; her recent prominence in the campaign to save the remains of the old Shakespearian theatre in London, the Rose, from the demands of property development has also shown her doggedness and her courage.

Rodrigo Moynihan's subtle portrait, her likeness captured with care but also with apparent lightness and fun, speaks of the personality of this least actressy of actresses. It gives us, we feel, the private person — still more remarkable is that she remains that person even in performance.

No. 11
Dame Peggy Ashcroft
1984, oil on canvas
71.2 x 55.8 cm
National Portrait Gallery, London
photograph: National Portrait Gallery

Humphrey Ocean
John Bickersteth, Bishop of Bath and Wells

The Church of England is the established national church in England. Its head is the Queen; its bishops are appointed by the Prime Minister, who chooses from a list of suitable candidates proposed by leading churchmen. In recent times eminent clergymen have occasionally spoken out against certain social policies and against government priorities, conveying a new sense of independence and a new urgency. It is difficult to estimate how many Britons are now regular church-goers and how many of these are true believers in the faith upheld by the Church. The beautiful parish churches and cathedrals that the new Church took over from the Roman Catholic Church in the sixteenth century live on as places of worship and focal symbols of the Church today, but also as strongholds of history.

We see the Bishop of Bath and Wells standing by the east end of Wells Cathedral, one of the finest ecclesiastical buildings in the land, built in the twelfth and thirteenth centuries. John Bickersteth was born in 1921, the son of a canon of the Church. After public school and study at Oxford he served in the British army during World War II and was ordained a priest in 1951. He was Bishop of Bath and Wells from 1975 to 1987, a thoughtful and caring shepherd of his ecclesiastical flock, known especially for his passion for and knowledge of church music. Humphrey Ocean has represented him as that shepherd. Like other traditional English portraits, this one shows a vertical emphasis in the figure and the picture format. See also Spear [No. 14], for another example of this preference. The rising lines of the cathedral reinforce this verticality, but we also feel that the weaving lines of the east window's tracery symbolize the polyphonic music John Bickersteth loves.

No. 12
John Bickersteth,
Bishop of Bath and Wells
1983, acrylic on canvas
182.9 x 76.2 cm
lent by courtesy of the
Lord Bishop of Bath
and Wells and the Church
Commissioners for
England
photograph:
Roger Perry, Somerset

Bryan Organ
Mr and Mrs Sharples

Organ's reputation is that of a reliable portraitist of royalty and others eminent in public life and of the stars of sport and popular music. Less well known but of at least equal interest are the portraits he paints for his own satisfaction. These can have a special degree of intensity, absent from his more public works, where the likeness of the sitter adds its own seduction.

Organ met Mr and Mrs Sharples when he visited Lancashire, in search of new subject matter. He was introduced to them by a man who raced whippets, and was captivated by their all-consuming passion for pigeons, which they kept in a loft in their back yard. They breed pigeons, test their homing skill by sending them far away to be released, and race them against others' cherished birds. The Sharples represent all such working-class people, who add this love and expertise to their otherwise more or less routine existence. We see the couple outside their pigeon loft, facing us with pride. Lit from the front, they are almost shadowless, as is the rest of the composition which, facing us, too, is an arrangement of flat or almost flat horizontal bands in front of which the Sharples hold court. (The pigeon held carefully in Mr Sharples' hands was named by them Bryan Organ.) This is realism, bearing a message about humanity, as well as naturalism, faithful transcription based on observation. Comparing it with the Tindle portrait [No.17] we may feel the absence of the poetic role Tindle gives to light and the humorous regard he shows for the sitter. Mr and Mrs Sharples may strike us more as types than as individuals carefully characterized. But Organ accords them great dignity, and that has its own poetry.

No. 13
Mr and Mrs Sharples
1975, acrylic on canvas
208.3 x 208.3 cm
collection of Richard Schlagman
photograph: Rodney Todd-White

Ruskin Spear
Baron Redcliffe-Maud

John Redcliffe-Maud became Baron Redcliffe-Maud in 1967, at the age of 61, in recognition of a distinguished career in the universities, in Parliament, and in public service. He was the son of a bishop, was educated at the public school, Eton College, and then at Oxford and Harvard. He became known first as a lecturer and writer on politics. From 1939 to 1943 he was Master of Birkbeck College, a branch of London University set up to enable people with day-time paid work, unable to afford higher education by other means, to study in the evenings and at the weekends for a range of degrees, and to pursue research. Then he became a civil servant, holding senior posts in several ministries. From 1961 to 1963 he was our ambassador to South Africa. He chaired many committees and was charged with preparing significant reports, including one on financial support for the arts in England and Wales (1976). He was the author of several noteworthy books on national and local government and on education. He died in 1982.

Spear's portrait, tall and narrow like the man himself, invites comparison with Ocean's portrait of the Bishop of Bath and Wells [No.12], but Redcliffe-Maud is shown with the barest of backgrounds and without any accessories other than the clothes he wears and the umbrella and briefcase he is carrying. Yet these say a lot. They are the identifying property of the professional gentleman of his time: black jacket and waistcoat, black-and-grey striped trousers, tightly rolled umbrella and a plain, undemonstrative case.

That is how Redcliffe-Maud arrived to sit for his portrait in Spear's studio. Spear had previously painted him wearing his gown and holding his regalia as Master of University College, Oxford. This is a much less formal image, the everyday man though still perhaps the public figure – not the private man with a passion for music and dancing. But we do see a man of intelligence and human sympathy, a humorous and lively individual. 'He was a marvellous chap', Spear has said; 'I enjoyed painting him'. Both parts of that statement are confirmed by this vivid painting.

No. 14
Baron Redcliffe-Maud
1984, oil on canvas
185.4 x 76.5 cm
National Portrait Gallery, London
photograph: National Portrait Gallery

Stanley Spencer
Portrait of Dame Mary Cartwright FRS Sc.D.

We associate the careful recording of detail that we see here with the North European tradition in painting that goes back to pictures produced in the Low Countries (the present Luxemburg, Netherlands and Belgium) around the fifteenth century and from then on. In this and other respects Stanley Spencer can certainly be seen as a northern painter. He observes sharply and delivers what he sees with a clarity that goes beyond our normal experience and thus seems emphatic, something more than mere realism. The fitment on the window frame draws from him the same degree of attention as his sitter's strong facial features and the material of her academic robes. Notice the imbalance of the eyes, exaggerated by the painter to strengthen the character of the image. Mary Cartwright was a leading British mathematician at a time when it was much rarer than it is today for women to become prominent in academic life and the sciences. She became a Fellow of the Royal Society in 1947. From 1961 to 1963 she was president of the London Mathematical Society. In 1969 she was honoured with the award of Dame Commander of the Order of the British Empire (DBE). She has also had many honorary doctorates and medals for her work, principally work on the theory of functions. Having been a Fellow of Girton College, Cambridge in the 1930s, from 1949 to 1968 she was Mistress of Girton, and it is in this role that Spencer was asked to portray her. She is seen here in her room at the College. The garden background was studied by Spencer from a different viewpoint than the sitter and her room, so that he could give the trees a strong presence in the picture. As so often in English portraits, vertical lines and forms dominate over horizontals.

No. 15
Portrait of Dame Mary Cartwright FRS, Sc.D.
1958, oil on canvas
76 x 49.5 cm
The Mistress and Fellows, Girton College,
Cambridge
photograph: Girton College, Cambridge

Graham Sutherland
Mark Longman

Graham Sutherland did not often paint portraits, but those he did paint have tended to become his best-known works on account of their dramatic forms and keen characterization. His painting of the writer Somerset Maugham was the first (1949) and led on to portrait commissions, including one for a portrait of the cosmetics tycoon Helena Rubinstein (1957). A remarkable event in British art was his being commissioned to do a portrait of Winston Churchill by a group of his parliamentary colleagues. They and the sitter disliked the result, and the painting was quietly destroyed by Churchill's family. Sutherland had produced a characteristic Sutherland portrait as well as a likeness that all could recognize instantly, but it did not sweeten the appearance or character of the gruff old man. The artist got a lot of public blame but the mistake was made by those who chose him to do the painting. His portrait of the publisher Mark Longman is also a convincing likeness. What could have been a tame representation of a good-looking man is given dramatic value by the way the figure is framed, imprisoned almost, in a structure of lines within the picture. Sutherland's painting technique is graphic rather than painterly and his portraits have a nervous sharpness that (as in the case of Spencer [No.15]) links him to the North European tradition.

No. 16
Mark Longman
1970, oil on canvas
143.5 x 104.8 cm
Longman Group
photograph: Longman Group,
Photographic Unit

David Tindle
Dirk Bogarde

The sitter, one of our best-loved film stars, has a house in the South of France. Tindle visited him there, to paint him in the place where he lives when he is not working, in a home he has made very much his personal environment. Yet this portrait's particular character comes in part from the fact that it tells us next to nothing about this home and makes no reference at all to the world outside (unlike, for example, Spencer's portrait of Mary Cartwright or Hambling's of Dorothy Hodgkin [Nos.15 and 7]) – except for that warm and gentle light that illuminates the sitter and floods the room, creating space and mood. We have no doubt that Bogarde inhabits a benign physical and spiritual world.

In fact, Bogarde sat to Tindle in a small upstairs bedroom: it is the painter, ignoring walls and corners and various items of constricting furniture, who invented the spacious setting of the portrait. Its horizontal format is relatively rare in English portraiture; it gives a sense of ease and expansiveness where a tall format might have added a sense of formality. A comparison with Graham Sutherland's painting [No.16], not unlike Tindle's in some respects, shows what complex messages we receive from the organization of a picture. The light-filled spaciousness of Tindle's composition is enhanced by his characteristic use of the old and delicate medium of egg tempera, applied in small touches and giving value to every part of the painting.

Dirk Bogarde has appeared on the stage and in films since 1947. He starred as the romantic lead in a series of comedies about young doctors, moving on to leading roles in dramatic films like *The Servant*. He gave perhaps his most remarkable performance in *Death in Venice* (1971), the film of Thomas Mann's famous short novel. He has himself written a number of successful novels, as well as three autobiographical volumes, published over the period 1977 to 1983. The painter asked him to wear that patterned jersey for the sittings: its diamonds echo the traditional costume of a centuries-old character on the popular European stage, Harlequin.

No. 17
Dirk Bogarde
1986, egg tempera on canvas
64.8 x 94.1 cm
National Portrait Gallery, London
photograph: National Portrait Gallery

Euan Uglow
Georgia

Art, in infinitely varied ways, shapes our response. Artists' voices are distinct even if they do not set out to be different, and different occasions may also inflect them, intentionally or not. Euan Uglow, like his teacher and friend William Coldstream [No.5] and like his colleague and friend Patrick George [No.6]), takes objective, dispassionate *looking* and makes it the system and process of his art. He chooses a subject – often a figure, sometimes a still-life motif – and makes deliberate dispositions for it: it must occupy a space clearly revealed in the painting, and it must occupy that space firmly, in clear relation to it.

Here Uglow has persuaded a friend to pose and he has related her very carefully to the seat with its geometrically patterned cushion, and to the background of door, door frame and wall. He has also been concerned with relating her and everything else to the edges of his canvas. There are also colour and tonal relationships to be decided on and watched. Every element must be given its sufficient visual presence in the composition. In making his image of Georgia with such care, Uglow accords her something close to goddess status: his painting brings to mind the austere and high-minded art of the great French painter of the French Revolution and the Napoleonic era, Jacques-Louis David, who sharpened and refined the classical tradition to give it renewed moral force. The forms in Uglow's painting are simplified yet retain enough detail to speak to us of facial expression, volume, texture, the living body beneath the clothes; they are also unassertive enough to enable us to assimilate the whole picture, the whole organization. The horizontal line we see most clearly to the left of Georgia, and which was evidently a design element from the start, lies half-way between the top and the bottom edge of the canvas. Georgia's left eye, the eye nearest us, is on the middle axis of the painting. Nothing is left undetermined and thus unvalued, yet there is nothing mechanical or hard about the image.

No. 18
Georgia
1973, oil on canvas
83.8 x 111.8 cm
The British Council
photograph: André Morain

Speaking portrayals

Frank Auerbach
John Bellany
Tony Bevan
Peter Blake
Eileen Cooper
Rose Garrard
Richard Hamilton
Patrick Heron
Susan Hiller
David Hockney
Allen Jones
Alexander Moffat
Leonard Rosoman
Jack Smith
Laetitia Yhap

Speaking portrayals

Likeness is not a prerequisite for this category; the extension of portrayal into discourse is. Moffat and Rosoman [Nos.30 and 31] do indeed catch a true likeness but go on to enlarge upon their sitters in a way that is not directly representational, setting them in context by reference to their work and interests. Garrard [No.24] reproduces a lifelike portrait as part of her enquiry into herself as woman and artist and into women's existence – the portrait is not her own likeness, although the other references in the work are autobiographical. Hamilton's apparently simple and direct self-portrait [No.25], a three-dimensional photograph which presents his image and refers to his profession, goes on to imply observations on art, creativity and sight. Two other self-portraits here give priority to self-revelation over self-portrayal. Bellany and Jones [Nos.20 and 29] use quite different means and distinct levels of gravity to speak about perplexities and admirations, in one case by clear representations of professional attachments and interests, in the other by more elliptical quotations and stylistic echoes that mirror processes of thought rather than their objects. In Hockney's and Cooper's paintings [Nos.28 and 23], we also meet quotations and symbols of various sorts, as well as an appearance of innocence and primitivism, as though these works were spontaneous, unrehearsed expressions of emotionally charged situations. All art, however, is partly about the making of art, and in the paintings of Auerbach, Heron and Bevan [Nos.19, 26 and 21] issues of image-making become dominant: Auerbach works to discover and rediscover a sense of someone's presence in his studio through a process that seems reluctant to refer directly to the sitter's appearance; Heron seeks an effective modern idiom in which to portray a great modern poet; Bevan achieves an unusually austere but also telling image.

What all these works demonstrate is humanity's inalienable need to look beyond surfaces and appearance in order to know and to understand. Some address us through epigrams, tersely; others are more loquacious. As in our social encounters, we respond to explanations and evaluations and also bring our own associations to bear on what we see, moving from the particular account offered to generalizations based on our own experience. Thus, Smith's lively child [No.32] becomes all children, and Hiller's awesome self-images [No.27] become images of us all.

Frank Auerbach
Catherine Lampert

The sitter emerges almost reluctantly out of the flux of oil paint and brushstrokes, out of apparent chaos. Auerbach paints as though there were no precedent to guide him, as though he had to invent anew each day how one might use paint on a flat surface to suggest the presence of a human being, and the tensions that this presence brings into the studio. He tends to paint the same subject again and again, reaching a kind of familiarity whilst discovering also the infinite variability given by light, distance, angle and perhaps also mood. Each painting requires many attempts and gets overpainted or scraped off and begun again. The final version springs from a climatic moment in this long labour and is usually carried out quickly, giving permanence to something experienced as immediacy. Because of this spontaneity and the aggressive appearance of Auerbach's brushstrokes – and thinking of his origins and early experiences – critics have been too ready to associate his work with that of the German Expressionists with their open emotionalism. What they do not notice is the patience with which Auerbach prepares the creative moment, his attachment to a powerful traditional formula in such a portrait as this one, and the clear, classical, geometric structure built with those brushstrokes. Order and chaos coexist in his work, as do the material form of the painting as object and the image inhabiting it.

Catherine Lampert, an art historian and sculptor, is now Director of the well-known municipal Whitechapel Art Gallery in the East End of London, after years in the art department of the Arts Council of Great Britain. She has sat at various times for Auerbach since 1970.

No. 19
Catherine Lampert
1983, oil on canvas
60 x 40 cm
private collection
photograph: Prudence Cuming Associates Ltd

John Bellany
Self-Portrait

Grave illness and a major operation recently brought
the painter close to death. This painting dates from early in
his slow recuperation and, like others of the time, is openly
introspective, a commentary as much as a portrayal. There
is an old Western tradition whereby the sitter's name and
sometimes age is written into portraits. Bellany has written
the date and the name of the great Venetian painter
Giovanni Bellini into his: a gesture of homage, as is the
reproduction of a Van Gogh self-portrait watching over him,
but the Bellini reference means more than that. We say
Bèllany; where he comes from in Scotland they say Bellàny.
Coming across Giovanni Bellini's work in Edinburgh as a
student, Bellany enjoyed the echo in their names. He knew,
also, that some centuries ago Italian ships had plied the
Atlantic route to Scotland, trading lava ballast for coal. Near
Bellany's school there still stands a wall constructed of
Italian lava. Might not the Bellanys be related to the
Bellinis?

He follows here a Bellini portrait formula, placing the
figure behind an inscribed parapet. The figure is masked.
(The cockerel is a Scots symbol and suggests strutting
youth.) He holds a famous Scottish book (literature) and an
accordion (music), and on the parapet lies a theatrical mask
(drama): paying homage to the arts. The clock and the mal-
evolent cat suggest time and the presence of dark spirits. I
see flames in the pattern on the wall and in Bellany's fine
blue cloak: conveying pain and damnation. Yet the image as
a whole speaks of survival.

GIOVANNI BELLINI. MARCH 87.

No. 20
Self-Portrait
1987, water - colour on paper
75.5 x 57.5 cm
loaned by IBM United Kingdom Limited
photograph: courtesy of Sarema Press
(Publishers) Ltd

Tony Bevan
Portrait of a Martyr

artist unknown
Sir Philip Sidney
oil on canvas
National Portrait Gallery
London

In a National Portrait Gallery exhibition, in 1985, this painting was hung next to a sixteenth-century portrait – of Sir Philip Sidney, courtier, soldier and outstanding writer of poetry, prose and criticism. Both paintings show a three-quarters figure against a dark background. Sidney stands there in an elegant, conventional pose, hand on hip, wearing his elegant, conventional clothes. Only his face could tell us possibly who he is, and that is simplified and idealized to bring out physical perfection, isolated from the rest of him by the elaborate ruff of starched and folded linen around his neck. Bevan's young man stands before us in a pose we may also think of as conventional because it is familiar, but it is familiar merely because it is ordinary, not a pose assumed for a portrait but just how people often look. The clothes, too, are conventional in this sense. The Sidney portrait is the product of small and careful brush-strokes making a compacted surface of colours and tones which we receive as a convincing representation of a human being. We think it realistic, but of course it is firmly abstracted and simplified. The anonymous man in Bevan's painting is presented as an exceptionally large drawing, without any of the shading or modelling that would suggest a three-dimensional object. This, and Bevan's spare use of paint and colour, gives the image an ascetic presence where the Sidney, for all its simplifications, is rich. Sidney is august, and the painting conveys that. Bevan's 'martyr' is ordinary, any young person, without status and probably without possessions. It is known that Bevan was stimulated to paint this figure through contact with the writing and biography of the French author Jean Genet, but he stresses that it is a form of self-portrait as well as a generalized image of Everyman. (A comparable fusion is found in Rose Garrard's composite work [No.24].) His mastery of line, by means of which alone he confronts us with so remarkably alive and sympathetic a figure, recalls the art of such nineteenth-century painters as Ingres and Degas, linking Bevan into the great Western tradition of classical art, just as the scale in which he presents the figure, well over life-size, associates it with Western images of gods and heroes. The austerity of the image suggests spirituality and transience where the Sidney portrait speaks of physical glamour and permanence.

No. 21
Portrait of a Martyr
1982, dry pigment, PVA
& charcoal on Triwall
190 x 114 cm
Arts Council Collection.
South Bank Centre,
London
photograph: John Webb
FRPS Photography

Peter Blake
Children Reading Comics

Blake's student works, of which this is an example,
were received with a mixture of shock and guarded
pleasure by critics and the general public. Today they are
admired by a wide public, and it is difficult to re-
experience the earlier shock. This art, surely, was vulgar.
Art's duty was to be high-minded, to promote aspirations
and embody the finest, most poetic responses to life and
nature. But this young man confronted us with a picture of
two children reading comics, and he even gave much of his
picture surface to describe that comic. The children are
frontal, the comic is frontal. Some of it is painted in a
careful, detailed way, exhibiting the painter's skill of eye
and hand, and some of it is vague, unfinished, thrown
away. Can this be art at all? Where is the elevating message?

'Why don't you paint pictures of what you like?' Blake
said to a student some years later. Painting what he liked
was paramount in Blake's scheme of things, and this
included many autobiographical subjects. The boy and girl
are young Peter and his sister Shirley, taken from photographs at a time when using a photograph for a painting
was more or less forbidden. Blake has also studied
fairground and circus art, and soon he was to embrace also
the imagery and the culture of American and British pop
music. Thus he was seen as one of the creators of the Pop
movement of the 1960s. Yet where other Pop artists were
eager to emulate and parody advertising design, Blake owed
more to selected aspects of the art he knew. There is
undoubtedly something of Stanley Spencer in his relish for
ordinariness [Nos.15, 55 and 56], and something of the then
professor of painting under whom Blake studied, Carel
Weight [No.61], in Blake's manner of painting.

No. 22
Children Reading Comics
1954, oil on hardboard
36.9 x 47 cm
Carlisle Museums and Art Gallery
photograph: Carlisle Museums and Art
Gallery

Eileen Cooper
Gift

The painting glows with colour and warm feelings. The colours in fact are few, but they are placed to bring out the resonance of each and allow contrasts that enhance their expression. Note, for example, the touches of gold in the woman's face and hair, and more predominantly also in her hands and in the child that lies there. More gold provides a kind of halo for the crescent moon. There is also a lot of blue, the opposite colour to gold, which complements the large quantity of red and is itself in places shot through with touches of red. Strong feeling comes also from the imagery, which is at once personal and of general human meaning. The 'gift' of the title is Eileen Cooper's first-born son. The child and the mother's face are generalized, and so he is all first-born children, representing the miracle of birth and, too, the moment when mothers are born. We see the father's face above the moon on the left. The moon is a female symbol, and the boat on the right may be seen both as a toy brought by friends or relatives for the child and as a symbol of time and of voyaging, of the journey embarked on by the new human being. The gold seems to radiate from him; for other reasons, too, it is natural for a Westerner to read this picture, consciously and unconsciously, in partly religious terms: it echoes the many images we see of the Nativity of Jesus Christ. (See also Rose Garrard's use of the Madonna and Child theme [No.24].)

Eileen Cooper's work is essentially autobiographical in that she draws directly on her personal experience, but she uses this experience poetically. She offers not detailed accounts of specific domestic scenes, as does Anthony Green [No.41], but concentrated and highly charged poetic images that give priority to the emotional value of the theme and lend it wide human significance. That painting should be used for such deeply personal and poetic expression is something relatively new to Western art. It came in with the Romantic movement of two hundred years ago and is a trend especially prominent and successful in British painting today.

No. 24
Orthodoxy: Rediscovering Laura Knight
1955 – 1987
1987, mixed media wall relief
104.1 x 69.9 cm
Louise Hallett Gallery, London
photograph: Miki Slingsby Fine Art
Photography

Richard Hamilton
Palindrome

The word 'palindrome' refers to a word or set of words that reads the same way backwards and forwards. Asked to contribute a work for an international set of prints on the theme of the mirror, Hamilton decided to offer a portrait of a mirror which would also be a portrait of an artist (himself) and comment on the complexities and perplexities of sight. But of course we cannot see mirrors; we deduce their existence. We see a blurred image of the artist. We see his hand and its mirror image: where the two fingers touch, marking the glass with paint, the photographic image is in true focus, both in the ordinary photographic sense and in the additional sense in which lenticular photography, which produces such a shifting appearance of three-dimensional life, has a secondary focus controlling the vertical bands of plastic prisms. Hamilton had great trouble getting the work done to the degree of perfection he required. He has used photography in other works, and is always concerned with the intellectual content of his processes, as well as his images. Art is a kind of mirror. We accept mirrors as useful items in daily life but they are also doorways into other worlds. They tell us untruths about ourselves. In Western art traditionally they signify vanity and warn us that what they show will pass; thus they are in league with time and breaking a mirror will bring seven years of bad luck. Everything Hamilton produces is compact with thought. I find in this work a reference to that most powerful image of creativity in Western art: the finger of God almost touching that of the newly created man, Adam, in Michelangelo's painted ceiling, charging humanity with energy and spirit. Yet Hamilton's figure simply shows the painter at work, doing his normal business.

No. 25
Palindrome
1974, lenticular acrylic laminated on collotype
72.5 x 57.1 cm
by courtesy of Waddington Graphics,
4 Cork Street, London W1
photograph: Prudence Cuming Associates Ltd

Patrick Heron
T S Eliot

Heron was a conscientious objector during World War II and was made to do 'useful' work in lieu of army service; because of this, he was not able to paint for six years, at the end of which he returned with especial urgency to his chosen task. In 1947 he asked Eliot for permission to do a portrait of him, and was allowed to come and make drawings of him where he worked at the publishers Faber and Faber. From this came three paintings and a finished drawing; this one is the climax of the series. In it Heron adopts the Cubist device of showing two views of the same object from different angles. The effect of seeing Eliot's face frontally and in profile is very strong. Heron has captured the poet's keen eyes and also the characteristic profile which someone described as 'like a bird of prey of some sort'. Notice that the painter has omitted all detail of the setting – unlike, say, Hambling in her portrait of Dorothy Hodgkin [No.7].

Eliot was one of the greatest and most widely read poets of modern times. He was born in America and came to Britain in 1914. By the 1920s he was generally regarded as the most important contemporary poet writing in English. His long and learned poem *The Waste Land* (1922) excited generations of young readers; his later poetry, notably his *Four Quartets*, speaks profoundly of spiritual experience. In 1948 he received Britain's most distinguished award for intellectual excellence, the Order of Merit, and was awarded also the Nobel prize for Literature. He died in 1965 at the age of seventy-six.

No. 26
T S Eliot
1949, oil on canvas
76.2 x 62.9 cm
National Portrait Gallery, London
photograph: Prudence Cuming Associates Ltd

Susan Hiller
Midnight, Baker Street

Susan Hiller's work with 'photomat' images is one part of her ongoing investigation of modern society. She pursues it as though she were a visitor from outside (she has at times worked as an anthropologist), questioning values and habits of thought. But of course she is a member of this society, and rightly investigates herself as well as others. She is a woman, and she offers what she has sometimes called the 'fruitful incoherence' of woman's natural discourse as an answer to the dominant male mode of 'rational' discourse, compartmented and sterile. The sheer variety of her work suggests that fruitful incoherence. Here she presents three enlarged 'photomat' images of herself. The originals were taken in an automat in Baker Street underground station in London: not the most comfortable of environments, especially at midnight. We see her face in three-quarters profile (looking at us/the camera), full face (with her eyes lowered) and in profile (looking left and up). In enlarging the image she has added strange colours and has also inscribed the faces with automatic writing which resists our attempts to decipher it. We try, too, to read the slightly out-of-focus faces, feeling the need to make contact with that human being. But the faces offer no certain signals. The writing is ornament, camouflage, veil. It demonstrates the sitter-artist's control, the taking-back of the image from the control of the machine. It asserts her hand and, through the calligraphic action, her thought, her right to expression. The unseen hand, we realize, is as important in establishing Hiller's being as her head. The title pointedly does not refer to herself but to urban existence: her image is everybody's.

No. 27
Midnight, Baker Street
1983, C-type photograph on Agfa-Lustre paper
3 panels each 71 x 51 cm
Arts Council Collection.
South Bank Centre, London
photograph: John Webb FRPS Photography

David Hockney
We Two Boys Together Clinging

This is one of the paintings with which Hockney came
before the public as a leading figure in what quickly
became known as Pop art, and as an outstanding new talent
in British art. He was still a student at the Royal College of
Art but his work, always skilful, had by now found a
markedly personal character in theme and manner, though
the latter echoed the graffiti, the scribbles on walls, which
is the folk art of city dwellers. It is one of a series of 'Love
Paintings' in which Hockney spoke poetically of homo-
sexual love, its pains and its joys, using words and cipher
that made his meaning clear to those who bothered to make
them out, at a time when male homosexuality had rarely
been treated in art. His chosen style enables him to be both
passionate and oblique. We see nothing that could offend
us, yet we know we are in the presence of strong feelings.
The title of the picture is a line from the great American
nineteenth-century poet, Walt Whitman; the words are
written boldly into the painting, and further lines from the
same poem can be found below the heart on the right. The
pair of primitively represented figures are the painter and
his friend; they have about them an ancient character that
hints at the timeless nature of the theme.

No. 28
We Two Boys Together Clinging
1961, oil on board
121.9 x 152.4 cm
Arts Council Collection.
South Bank Centre, London
photograph: courtesy Arts Council Collection.
South Bank Centre, London

Allen Jones
The Artist Thinks

Among the young painters who became known as Pop
artists in London at the start of the 1960s, Allen Jones stood
out for his particularly intelligent and thoughtful approach
to image-making and for the elegance of the results. I take
The Artist Thinks to be an assertion as much as the title of
this indirect self-portrait. Artists think: of course they do,
but the world needs reminding of it, so prevalent is the
notion that art is thoughtless expression of emotion when it
is not a direct mirroring of the visible world. Conscious
thought is often said to prevent any authentic artistic
statement. Jones's art proposed – at a time when British
painting meant primarily the St Ives School of expressive
landscape abstractionists and the cool and apparently
content-less hard-edge canvases of the Situation group –
an intensely personal vision that was at the same time
wholly contrived and refused to be limited by demarcations
between figuration and abstraction. His poetic image of
himself, and of the thoughts that loom over him in a great
bubble, refers us to art, notably to Kandinsky's work which
he particularly admired (though at that time the Russian/
German/French painter's stock did not stand as high as it
does today), and refers us also to other visual information
(for example, the arrow), as well as generally to the world of
advertising.

No. 29
The Artist Thinks
1960, oil on canvas
121.9 x 121.9 cm
the artist
photograph: courtesy of Allen Jones

Alexander Moffat
Hugh MacDiarmid. Hymn to Lenin

Moffat considers MacDiarmid 'without doubt the greatest Scottish artistic thinker of the twentieth century'. MacDiarmid (1892-1978) was indeed a vigorous poet and essayist. If he has relatively few admirers in England, it is because he was fiercely anti-English and pro-Scots. He condemned the English domination over Celtic culture as an aspect of British imperialism. He was also a passionate socialist. For him the Russian Revolution was by far the greatest event in modern times. He was a member of the Communist Party most of his life, and he fed into his writings the wide knowledge that Lenin said was the necessary equipment of all communists. He read in and translated from several European languages, especially German and Russian.

Moffat's portrait started from studies done in MacDiarmid's home shortly before his death, but developed into something more complex: a likeness that is also an account of him as thinker and worker. We see the writer seated in his armchair, elderly and energetic. The gesture of his right hand indicates speech. A book is open beside him. The figure just emerging below the book is the great Scots socialist John Maclean, a Leninite figure in the history of Scotland. We see Lenin himself in the middle of the painting, next to a summary glimpse of a British policeman on a horse. Below Lenin is a group of Russian revolutionaries in a lorry, storming the Tsar's palace in Petrograd in 1917. The two men shown to the right of that are Lunacharsky, playwright and Commissar for Education and the Arts in the new Soviet state, and the great popular poet Mayakovsky. The structure of which we glimpse the top behind Mayakovsky represents the famous monument designed to stand in Petrograd and function as the head-quarters for the organization of world revolution, invented and exhibited as a large model by the artist Vladimir Tatlin in 1920-21; the real thing was to have been a hundred metres higher than the Eiffel Tower in Paris. The landscape in the background is Moffat's synthetic account of parts of Scotland where MacDiarmid lived.

No. 30
Hugh MacDiarmid. Hymn to Lenin
1981, oil on canvas
109.5 x 188.5 cm
Scottish Arts Council Collection
photograph: Scottish Arts Council

Leonard Rosoman
Lord Esher in the Studio

Lord Esher, a well-known architect and author, retired from the directorship of the Royal College of Art in London in 1978. There is a tradition at the College whereby retiring rectors (as they are called there) are recorded for posterity by means of a formal portrait. Esher was reluctant to do that. What is more, Leonard Rosoman, who had been asked to consider doing the required painting, was not happy about doing anything so predictable. Over a succession of social meetings, the two of them agreed that it might be possible to do a portrait of a very informal sort – thus, a portrait only in part but a picture that fits the sitter and informs us about him whilst also indirectly accommodating the interests of the painter.

In the event, the portrait as such is entirely convincing: there is no problem about recognizing that slim, elegant but also unselfconscious figure and that sensitive head. Behind him, on the easel, we are shown a large landscape painting. It represents Kensington Gardens (part of Hyde Park) as they would appear when seen from the top floor of the College building next to the Royal Albert Hall. The Gardens were very much part of Esher's life at the College. In difficult moments he would go for a stroll through them, to refresh himself and clear his mind. But the painting we see within the painting is entirely a fiction, invented by Rosoman for the portrait. The view through the windows to the left is a simplified account of the buildings he sees from his studio elsewhere in London. The intense blue sky gives them a distinctly Mediterranean flavour. So the painting as a whole is largely fictitious, and its official title is partly untrue. The delicacy and wit of the picture are typical of Rosoman, who is a fine draughtsman as well as an acute judge of colour (note the effect of the lilac carpet) and of slightly eccentric compositions.

The painter says that producing this portrait was a major event in his career: he subsequently painted a number of pictures that are in part portraits and in part accounts of particular environments and occasions. He has thus accidentally but happily become a modern contributor to a type of English portrait sometimes known as the 'conversation piece' and often showing two or more figures in a relaxed, informal situation.

No. 31
Lord Esher in the Studio
1978, acrylic on canvas
122 x 152 cm
Royal College of Art Collection
photograph: Royal College of Art

Jack Smith
Child Walking with Check Tablecloth

In the 1950s Jack Smith was a leading figure in what one critic dubbed – thinking particularly of Smith's paintings – the Kitchen Sink School. The label implied something more than realistic art, pointing to the emphatically unglamorous realities of everyday domestic life. In fact, the work done by this so-called school varied both in style and in preferred subject matter. In Smith's case we were certainly struck by his use of low, earthy colours and his strong tonal contrasts, by his dramatic silhouettes and foreshortenings, as well as by his (as they then struck us) charmless themes. There is a tradition of working-class realism in North European art from at least the seventeenth century on, some of it done for moralizing purposes, some of it to amuse better-off picture collectors. Here, there is no sense of the painter keeping himself at any social distance from his subject. Rather he engages with it totally, without prejudice, valuing the vividness of every part of the subject, most of all the intense life of the little child, eagerly taking its first steps over the kitchen floor. Decades have passed since Smith painted this – and he has meanwhile turned to a personal form of clear-cut abstract art, with sharp little forms not unlike writing often set on a crisp white ground. The earlier painting now reveals qualities of elegance that were not so apparent in the 1950s: the colour is richer than it then seemed and the forms are rigorously shaped and assembled. There is something characteristically northern about Smith's liking for sharp detail (in different ways also apparent in the paintings of Spencer [Nos.15, 55 and 56] and of Sutherland [No.16]) but this does not override a dramatic sense of form and of space, so that there is marked emphasis on the presence and energy of the child.

No. 32
Child Walking with Check Tablecloth
1953, oil on board
153 x 122 cm
The British Council
photograph: Rodney Todd-White

Laetitia Yhap
Paul, Michael, Stephen and Tim in Summer

Five young men form a foreground frieze, lithe figures made to seem even slimmer by being silhouetted against the sea. Four of them are busy clearing a fish-net. Above their heads seagulls wheel about noisily, ready to swoop on food. One of the men (the unnamed one?) sits and watches, not unlike the painter herself, outside the picture. By his feet, a dog scratches itself.

Describing it in this way makes it seem a naturalistic picture, a detailed account of something closely observed. But it is also something more. It seems to me to embody a precious vision. The form of the painting itself proposes that. A rectangular format would certainly make the scene look more ordinary. Its roughly oval shape, the work of a handyman rather than a fine cabinet- or frame-maker, suggests an enshrining of what is represented instead of the familiar window view that we get through a frame. There is a fair amount of detail, so that we can read every part, but not so much as to interfere with our seeing the picture as a whole. When we do so, we are moved by Laetitia Yhap's disposition of light and dark, the relatively dark foreground contrasting with the partly light-reflecting surface of the water. An additional luminosity on the water towards the horizon introduces a supernatural note. We may not choose to think of the birds as spirits or angelic visitors, but there is something about them that suggests another world. Murfin's painting [No.49] makes an interesting comparison, more factual, more detailed, but also imparting value through its treatment of a similar subject.

No. 33
Paul, Michael, Stephen and Tim in Summer
1977–79, oil on board with sand
122.4 x 143 cm
Arts Council Collection.
South Bank Centre, London
photograph: John Webb FRPS Photography

Actions, stories, declarations

John Bellany
Boyd and Evans
P J Crook
Ken Currie
Joan Dawson
Mark Fairnington
Amanda Faulkner
Anthony Green
Peter Griffin
Peter Howson
Andrzej Jackowski
Ken Kiff
Leon Kossoff
Jock McFadyen
Bruce McLean
Michael Murfin
Tom Phillips
David Redfern
Paula Rego
Ceri Richards
William Roberts
Stanley Spencer
Peter Unsworth
Michael Upton
Keith Vaughan
Carel Weight

Actions, stories, declarations

This is the category that has seen such surprising development in the 1980s. Twentieth-century avant-garde art had tended away from narrative and discourse: it said things about the human situation but fed them into signs and symbols. Now there is a renewed interest in using art as a way of delivering more easily read statements. As a result, greater attention is now paid to traditions of pictorial narrative, and especially to artists such as Stanley Spencer who always gave priority to this kind of work.

Pictures being non-sequential, narrative painting demands a prepared, or at least partially prepared, viewer. Perhaps we can make out quite easily what is going on in Green's, Roberts' and Unsworth's pictures, helped by their titles [Nos.41, 54 and 57]. We can imagine ourselves in the company of the people in Boyd and Evans's or Crook's reports [Nos.35 and 36]. But what if we do not know the story of Echo and Narcissus, invoked by Kiff [No.45], or any of the implications of Jackowski's tacit drama [No.44]? Is it essential to know Phillips' particular ways of finding and promoting pre-existing images [No.50]? Knowledge helps, and on the pages that follow some information is offered. But more important is the attention we bring to art. Information can unlock the door; full admission to these images requires a responsiveness which comes from sensitivity to the various modes used by the artist and from looking into our own store of experience. In some cases the content is much more open-ended than in others. Green's autobiographical scene is quite clear and specific, though it may lead us to think of the role of childhood memories in adult life. Jackowski's image, also in part autobiographical, associates personal memories with the wider world of history and of myth. Rego's amazing, half-familiar images [No.52] draw us into speculations of all sorts, and their powerful expression will not let us pass by. We listen both to what the picture is saying, and to how it says it. Other painters are intent on delivering quite specific messages, and today these are often about labour and social justice. The message is at times implicit, as in Dawson's firm and loving account of steelworkers [No.38] or in Upton's surreptitiously challenging paired images [Nos.58 and 59], but it can also be a form of public rhetoric, as in Currie [No.37]. Here, size, formal presentation and an assertive idiom make for a memorable, compelling image. A similar purpose, I suggest, is served through less exhortatory means in Kossoff's [No.46] affectionate account of young bodies disporting themselves so energetically in the plain environment of an old municipal swimming-pool.

John Bellany
Chinatown

London Transport has an excellent tradition of commissioning work from prominent artists to advertise its services. John Bellany's poster, a reproduction of this painting, has been outstandingly successful in a current advertising campaign. One sees it again and again in Underground stations, and its vividness combined with the appeal of its subject and its artfulness hold one's attention every time.

Bellany likes going in to London's Chinatown. He likes the restaurants there, but also finds them places of enduring mystery and magic. There is some strangeness in his picturing of this scene: a table seen from above, around it two elegant Chinese women and two Chinese men, and, nearest to us, a Western woman; on the table there is food but also a game of draughts and the placing of playing cards. We may make of it what we will. It adds up to a powerful and enticing image of an aspect of Chinese life in Britain, thanks partly to its linear structure and its coloration, and especially to its concentration of the space required by the table and the people into an emphatically two-dimensional representation.

Chinatown
by Underground
nearest station Leicester Square

中國城

Chinatown
John Bellany ARA

one of a series commissioned
by London Underground

No. 34
Chinatown
1987, oil on canvas
127 x 157.5 cm
loaned by London Underground Ltd
photograph: London Underground Ltd

Boyd and Evans
Golden Wedding

Boyd and Evans' typical paintings are disquieting: they are highly realistic images, based on photographs, compiled and composed to imply danger or problems. This one is exceptional, in this and other respects. It is a record of a party given to celebrate a fiftieth wedding anniversary in the Boyd family. A lot of family and friends came together convivially under a marquee. They chatted, ate and drank, made and listened to speeches in praise of the occasion. No hidden drama, no disrupting of our habitual reading of the world. Instead, we see a group of people portrayed as they were that day, a collection of heads and shoulders. One of the traditional difficulties about a group portrait is that painters have sooner or later to attend to each individual in it in turn, normally posing and painting them in the studio, then fitting them into a setting and composition that will give the impression of a social event. Boyd and Evans used a video camera for this work. They could presumably have panned around the assembled company and then reproduced what the camera saw. They preferred to use the video material as stills, one head at a time, arranging the thirty plus portraits in a loose, rhythmic sequence, made decorative but also tidy by the device of the three parallel bands. Some people are shown more than once. Our first impression is of a lot of people enjoying themselves together. Gradually we sense their separateness. Boyd and Evans have not struggled to pretend that they have painted the party as it actually was, with people interacting naturally. The groupings they have invented on the basis of the camera's record do suggest a busy crowd of people and give a lively effect to the whole work, but it is perhaps characteristic of them that the triple frieze of heads soon reveals itself as a synthetic arrangement. The oil medium they used is oil sticks, giving a limited colour range but permitting some mixing of colours on the surface. The soft focus was given by the video camera. The smooth, enveloping light is sunshine dispersed by the canvas of the marquee. The painting was completed quite quickly, within a month of the event.

No. 35
Golden Wedding
1988, oil on canvas
3 images each 35 x 213 cm
property of D E and P F Tatham
photograph: Adrian Flowers

P J Crook
29th September 1988

This is a vivid and a familiar scene. The British, it
seems, read more newspapers than anyone else, and we are
used to seeing people standing in railway and underground
stations, waiting for trains and immersed in their daily
newspaper. But it is not a naturalistic picture. P J Crook is
often spoken of as a primitive painter, and the way she
represents persons as types rather than individuals – also
the way she shows all those heads full-face, in profile or in
three-quarters profile, avoiding the infinite variations a
more skill-conscious painter might want to demonstrate –
does indicate a kind of simplicity. But simplification of this
sort gives her image a timeless character and makes it
represent us all, as is true also of William Roberts' picture
of people and buses [No.54]. This generalizing effect is
contradicted by the attention she pays to the newspapers.
They are portrayed so exactly that we can tell which is
which even if we cannot see the masthead, and of course
papers necessarily lack this generality, being tied to a
particular day. So what seemed a very simple and naïve
presentation gradually reveals complexities. The way Crook
constructs space adds another intricacy. The foreground
heads are larger than the more distant ones, and this,
together with the evident overlapping of forms, speaks of
the space in which these people and their papers exist. We
feel she has crowded them into it, implying also that the
crowd continues outside the area shown. But there is also a
sense of air and movement, of intervals rather than tight
compression, and this is suggested by her use of the corrugated surface, because of which her forms shift a little as we
ourselves move.

No. 36
29th September 1988
1988, oil on corrugated wood panel
91.4 x 127 cm
courtesy Portal Gallery Ltd, London W1
photograph: Portal Gallery

Ken Currie
In the City Bar ...Disillusion

It is rare for British art to display open polemics. This has something to do with our long attachment to the classical tradition of Greece and Rome and the moderation it calls for, and, too, with the English insistence on the arts as a form of polite communication, governed by conventions of good manners. Currie is a Scot, trained and working in Glasgow like his friend Peter Howson [No.43]. Currie has long admired Hugh McDiarmid, the Scots scourge of English domination represented in Moffat's painting [No.30]. He is following McDiarmid's call for Scots voices and political themes, but has had to find a visual language for it. He has found it in a variety of foreign models, assimilated over the years: Rivera and the other Mexican muralists: Léger, the great French painter of modern humanity; the plays and poems of Brecht; the great film-makers, especially Eisenstein. We can see their influence in this large drawing, but should notice also a fundamental ambiguity in its image, reflecting the artist's refusal to speak in simplistic terms. Currie has a keen sense of positive and negative forces in Western industrial society. There are those making for fuller consciousness in everybody and leading to reform; there are those that hold mankind down, notably oppressive living and working conditions, but also drink, ritualized violence as entertainment, and so on. We glimpse these in the photographs on the wall of this bar; the bar itself is a dangerous gathering-place. Its customers, represented energetically, show both submission and defiance. The composition as a whole, with its rising diagonals and other sloping lines, speaks of hope and is dominated by the arm and clenched fist of the man at its centre. The date written on the table, 1690, refers to key events in the history of Scotland's union with England.

No. 37
In the City Bar... Disillusion
1985, conte pencil on paper
238.8 x 152.4 cm
Leeds City Art Galleries
photograph: West Park Studios, Leeds

Joan Dawson
Heroes

The painting's dimensions, as well as its title, spell out
its message unambiguously. These men, steelworkers, are
heroes. Dawson pursues her work as painter by working
among them, in sympathy with them; she is equally well-
informed about the machines they master and the processes
men and machines collaborate in. Her picture celebrates
them all, and it is worked cleanly, without any of the rhet-
orical gestures of technique, colouring or composition that
would draw attention to the painter's intervention between
subject and viewer. She wants her work to be accessible and
meaningful to the kind of people she portrays in it. The
image reports truthfully on the scene, but it is also clear
that, in painting the men, she has sharpened her realistic
idiom, simplifying the forms and also dramatizing them,
especially the strong, determined faces. The nearer figure in
fact represents her father, who had worked at such a drop-
forge for fifty years before being made redundant. So there
is a sub-plot which the image itself does not reveal: the
main hero, the man demonstrating his skill and experience
in setting the hot steel element into the forge, has actually
been thrown out of work, deprived of his heroic role in the
name of economic efficiency. The worker and the economic
system within which he operates are shown to be at odds.
The slight difference in treatment of the men and the
machine hints at this duality.

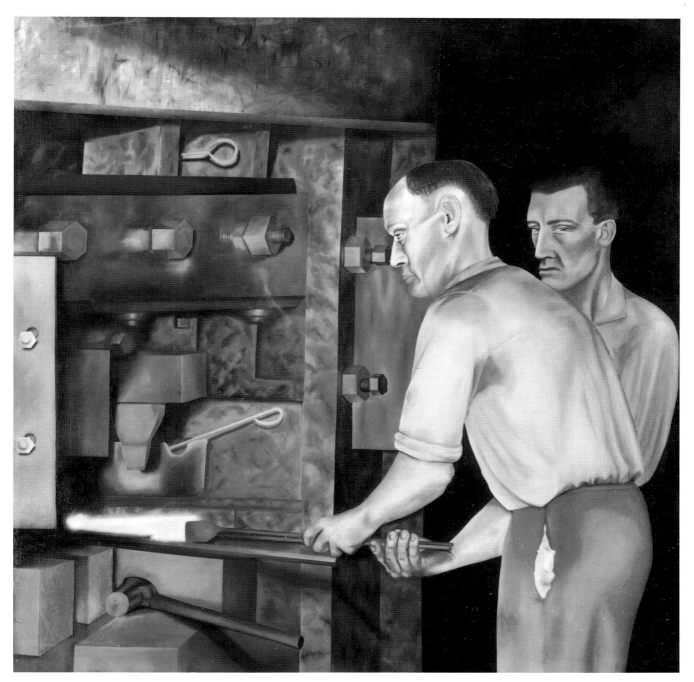

No. 38
Heroes
1982 – 83, oil on canvas
167.6 x 167.6 cm
Joan Heather Dawson
photograph: Rodney Todd-White

Mark Fairnington
The Rotten Aubergine

We live in a multicultural society, guided by diverse conventions. This concentrated picture exemplifies our ethnic problems in the form of a miniature comedy of manners. We British are not supposed to handle the goods offered in shops and on market stalls. But other people do. Here an Indian lady, identified not only by her sari but also by the style in which her profile is painted, echoing Indian art, is fingering the aubergines on a stall and has found one to be rotten. The stall-holder glares at her from the left; another man, probably an immigrant from the Middle East, watches to see how the incident will end.

The whole scene has been presented in decorative as well as unusually direct terms. Fairnington shows the stall's wheels spread-eagled to right and left. The two men are projected into the picture from the sides; we have no idea where they are standing, and there is no certain top or bottom to the composition. We seem to look down on the stall and its wares, enumerated with a child's attention, so that it is of course against naturalistic logic to show the woman in profile. Every part is full of colour and pattern. The decorative ensemble is reinforced by the border, which suggests that the whole thing is a carpet or hanging. There is a precedent for this in modern Western painting but it refers us back to Oriental traditions.

No. 39
The Rotten Aubergine
1986, acrylic on paper
61 x 91 cm
The British Council
photograph: Rodney Todd-White

Amanda Faulkner
Upright Women

The work of Amanda Faulkner, like that of Eileen Cooper and Rose Garrard [Nos. 23 and 24], is often labelled 'feminist'. That label is correct in that her work deals with human issues from the woman's point of view and stems from her own individual experience as a woman, exploring and illuminating the incompatibility of that experience and the stereotyped roles offered to women in what is still a male-dominated society. But none of these artists would want to be thought narrowly polemical. Their concern is to enhance understanding, not build barriers within it.

Faulkner came to professional art training late, after a period in South America where she lived among the Indian peoples of the Andes. Her English experience there confronted quite different priorities and behaviour – 'how they took care of one another, how they lived in that harsh environment with music and poverty and violence and death'. Then she worked and travelled in Europe. When she did go to art school she found her intense personal imagery frowned on by tutors looking for abstract compositions. For some time she worked mainly as a graphic artist, producing drawings and prints. During the last five year she has worked also on a much larger scale, and *Upright Women* shows an eloquent combination of graphic signs with painterly qualities. Her themes are fairly constant: women, woman as mother, woman as lover, woman's desire for individual recognition and recognition of the demands made on her. In this painting two crowned women consider the urgings of a man. The woman in the middle carries a child in her womb. The way this is shown and the organization of the image as a whole suggest traditions of medieval icon painting, giving a religious intensity to what at the same time is a very direct and personal expression of thoughts and feelings.

No. 41
Christmas Mirror 1947
1982, oil on board
198 x 284.5 cm
The British Council
photograph: courtesy Sainsbury Centre
for Visual Arts

Peter Griffin
The Tackle

In Rugby football the player carrying the ball can be stopped by the opposing player by a physical action: he can be knocked down or pulled down to the ground. This tackle is the subject of Peter Griffin's painting. Two men in yellow jerseys are grabbing at a man in a striped jersey. They are not distinguished otherwise: just three stocky males, with mighty arms and legs, and faces made to seem more tough by the facets of green, brown and turquoise that interrupt their flesh tint. Hatching adds to the sense of toughness. At the same time, the tackle is represented as a flat image, a designed knot of bodies with little mass and no space. (Compare Griffin's idiom with that of William Roberts [No.54].) In the bottom left corner of Griffin's painting we see one of the flags set up to mark the corner of the pitch; above that we see a fragment of lettering, part of an advertisement beyond the edge of the pitch.

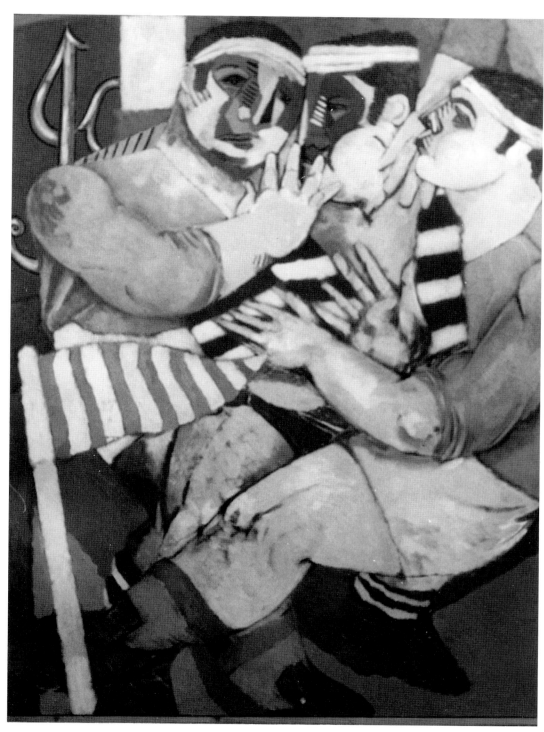

No. 42
The Tackle
1980, oil on canvas
121.9 x 91.4 cm
Nigel Llewellyn, Brighton
photograph: Rodney Todd-White

Peter Howson
Lowland Hero Spurns the Cynics

Howson's narrative is as open-ended as it is dramatic. He is himself a strongly built man and there are many other such in Glasgow, some of them socially deprived and sometimes physically damaged individuals, gathering in the area of Glasgow where Howson has his studio. The 'Hero' of this picture has aspects of them and also of himself: a mighty presence charged with something he wants to say to the people in the street. He has the urgency and the passion but we cannot be sure that he has found the words. He and the sky, certainly, have the painting's colour; the others are almost colourless and without character. Yet what is happening to him? He stands on a raised area of some sort, protected or confined by railings, and we are reminded of the carts which once carried condemned people to public execution. Does he know what is happening? He looks up into the sky, his ally. His face, his muscular arms and expressive hands speak to us without coherence. Over his shoulder hangs a plaid which could be a bag holding his possessions or perhaps part of a set of Scottish bagpipes. His energy is also the energy of the painting: the sometimes vehement, sometimes surprisingly delicate brushwork, the low viewpoint which makes him loom over us and the townscape, the dynamism of every part. The picture is a powerful visual statement that, like Jackowski's [No.44], refuses to explain itself fully and thus compels us to work with it. If one of the functions of the 'Hero' is to represent Howson, then it can be read as a comment on the long and continuing tradition whereby Scottish artists had to leave Scotland to build a successful career; Howson and a few others have recently broken this habit, working in Glasgow and becoming known in Britain and abroad as Glasgow painters.

No. 43
Lowland Hero Spurns the Cynics
1985, oil on canvas
213.4 x 152.5 cm
Scottish Arts Council Collection
photograph: Sean Hudson

Andrzej Jackowski
Earth-Stepper with Running Hare

Jackowski's paintings are rich visually and rich in the thoughts they offer. They draw on his personal experience, factual and imaginary, and from mythical material consonant with it. This painting was stimulated by Michel Tournier's novel *The Erl-King*, the hero of which, carried by a powerful friend in boyhood, discovers in himself a longing and a duty to carry others – an inversion of fascism's progress, boots marching over the bodies of millions. The long hut in Jackowski's painting represents oppression and homelessness, and denies us a horizon. The running hare is an image of life and energy: Jackowski says he only once saw one, and that was in his native Poland. He and his parents were displaced persons in postwar Europe. In London, aged twelve, he marvelled at Pisanello's intense representation of *The Vision of St Eustace* in the National Gallery, and found in it a similar hare. Jackowski has a daughter, yet it would be simplistic to see the two figures as a generalized double portrait. The image represents them but also many others and much else as the alert man carries the child in search of a possible future. Their closeness and frontality, the line of the hut, the white glow in the sky and the warm white ground, the hare's path between – all these make for a strange pictorial space and a particular poetry. It is a painting about fortitude more than about suffering.

No. 44
Earth-Stepper with Running Hare
1987, oil on canvas
152 x 234 cm
Marlborough Fine Art (London) Ltd
photograph: Prudence Cuming Associates Ltd

Ken Kiff
Echo and Narcissus, Sequence 81

Since 1970 Kiff has been devoting part of his output to what he calls his 'sequence' of smallish paintings. To us they are not significantly different from his other paintings; for him they hold a special place in his work. There are nearly two hundred of them now. They start from his imagination and embody waking and dreaming experiences. If one asks him what the sequence is about, half expecting him to describe it as a form of self-examination, a sort of metaphorical autobiography, he tends to answer in terms of art alone. In this he reveals an ambition to stand beside the great masters he admires so much, studies again and again, and speaks (and sometimes writes) about so wisely. These are modern masters and old masters, and it is not only Western art he is concerned with: recently, for example, he formed a passionate interest in Chinese painting. He says he wants to make paintings that are about the various energies of colour, of shapes, of brushstrokes, of space and interval, as much as about the imagery and actions they present.

A few of the paintings in the sequence were instigated by pictures he admires. *Echo and Narcissus* is quite unlike the great French painter's treatment of the same subject (in the Louvre Museum, Paris). For one thing, Poussin gives a much fuller account of the ancient myth related by Ovid and other Roman writers: Narcissus fell in love with his own reflection, whereas the nymph Echo pined away and died for unrequited love of him. Kiff invokes the story for its elegiac character but is not concerned to relate it fully. He cherishes it partly because, like others of its kind, it has lived on through the centuries to become an active element in the modern world's inheritance. Ken Kiff manifestly holds art and all poetic expression in high esteem; it is one of the virtues of contemporary British painting that the example set by Kiff has had such marked influence.

No. 45
Echo and Narcissus, Sequence 81
1977, acrylic on paper
66.3 x 52.3 cm
Arts Council Collection.
South Bank Centre, London
photograph: Eileen Tweedy Photography

Leon Kossoff
Children's Swimming Pool, Autumn 1972

Kossoff is a grave and meditative painter. He generally paints single figures but recently he has also painted street scenes and such public places as this London swimming-pool, of which he has done a number of pictures. His paintings assert that they are made of paint: as with the work of Frank Auerbach [No.19] we see a surface of paint as much as a representation. But whereas Auerbach, working with paint into a surface of paint, is using a process to create a surface close to relief sculpture, Kossoff remains more the visual painter, establishing with his colours and marks a very particular and complex experience. In this sense, especially in this series, he is a latter-day Impressionist. His painting, perhaps not easy to read at first glance, soon reveals its subject and, as it does so, tells us a great deal about it in ways we easily recognize. The space of the swimming-pool is clearly described. The little bodies become self-evident once we are content to see the swarm – just as one would in real life, entering such a place – and do not attempt to distinguish each individual child. What the painting delivers with almost painful directness is the sheer hubbub of an indoor pool full of young humanity, bringing sharply to mind one's own unfocused, dizzy experience of such a place. The clear spatial organization and the sense of local detail keep our eyes moving over the whole painting, and this again allows us to associate this work with the tradition of Impressionism rather than with the Expressionism with which some critics prefer to associate Kossoff's work.

No. 46
Children's Swimming Pool, Autumn 1972
1972, oil on board
182.9 x 213.4 cm
Arts Council Collection.
South Bank Centre, London
photograph: Photo Studios Ltd

Jock McFadyen
With Singing Hearts, Throaty Roarings...

This picture tells of the young men who crowd into
football matches up and down the country and use these
occasions for displays of hooliganism, often under the
influence of drink. The primitive conditions still offered by
some football clubs to their spectators are part of the problem, but there are also deeper social flaws that produce this
behaviour. There has been wide debate, in Parliament and
in the media, as to what should be done.

McFadyen's lively and vividly painted collage shows us
heads and hands, almost exclusively. There is a surprising
historical precedent for this kind of concentration – in
sixteenth-century religious paintings by Dürer much the
same use was made of caricature. Here a young man kisses
his girl in the centre of the picture; a youth on the right
spits at their amorous display while another shouts at them.
The white lettering says 'ALE', advertising a beer. The
Union Jack has been brought to the match, so it may be that
the picture refers to a match between a British and a foreign
team, occasions when some of the worst violence has
occurred. Here there is no violence as yet, merely uncouth
behaviour and a sense of dereliction. McFadyen's style owes
much to the modern urban folk art of graffiti, and his rough
and ready use of the collage technique produces a sense of
vulgarity, as though he were describing the scene in the
crude language of the people he is representing.

No. 47
With Singing Hearts, Throaty Roarings…
1983, collage
178 x 118 cm
The Trustees of the Imperial War Museum
photograph: Imperial War Museum (Art)

Bruce McLean
The Throw, The Post, The Bananas, The Tray

Bruce McLean, whose training was principally in sculpture, is best known as a performance artist, offering himself and at times a team of collaborators as a transient work of art, pointedly ironic as well as entertaining. This description (aside from 'transient') fits also the paintings he has been doing recently. There is an element of performance in the way they are painted, with intentionally wild gestures working against his strong linear design, so that the handling of the paint seems to be in conflict with the subject, the performer at odds with the scriptwriter. The subject remains elusive, although we seem to be offered access to it through the key words provided in the title and scribbled into the picture's margins. Here, too, we sense conflict, between the scribbled words and the final title shown on the label beside the painting and printed here.

The situation appears to be public, on stage and lit by theatrical lighting, so that this painting is, it seems, at least in part about performing and the special world inhabited by performers. Why do we look up to them and to their world so readily? 'The Throw' refers to the figure to the left, the ancient *Discobolus* mentioned and illustrated in connection with Bowyer's painting [No.2]. Under the other spotlight we can make out a typical pair of ballroom dancers going through absurd, falsely expressive motions. To their right is a column, perhaps 'The Post'. 'The Bananas' may refer to the green growth behind the discus-thrower and 'The Tray' to the rectangular picture as such, relating it to the decoration of painted trays. We are left to find whatever logic we can in all this, or indeed to do without, carried along by the vivacity of the execution.

No. 48
The Throw, The Post, The Bananas, The Tray
1980, acrylic and oil pastel on paper
143.5 x 180 cm
The British Council
photograph: Jörg P Anders

Michael Murfin
Farriery Competition II

Many people in the West feel they are losing touch with the countryside. We are cooped up in towns and cities while large-scale intensive farming has limited our access to the natural environment. Perhaps because of this, we treasure landscape and rustic activities as ideals of a better life. The rise of landscape painting and pictures of country life followed upon the heels of the industrial revolution that turned these same scenes into another world, a remote paradise, touched with nostalgia.

Blacksmiths hold an especially important place in our mythology of the countryside. Horses have not been driven out entirely by the internal-combustion engine, and horses need horseshoes. Michael Murfin's painting shows two men at an agricultural exhibition, competing with others in the making and fixing of horseshoes efficiently and quickly, using much the same tools and processes as were used centuries ago. The painter's sympathetic account of the scene owes its accuracy to photography and its formal strength to the traditions of classical composition in Western painting.

No. 49
Farriery Competition II
1988, acrylic on canvas
61 x 76.2 cm
Piccadilly Gallery, London W1
photograph: Rodney Todd-White

Tom Phillips
Conjectured Picture, Mappin Art Gallery, Sheffield, No.6

The beautiful, dreamy scene appears to be one of
elegant people spending a leisurely afternoon under trees, a
group portrait perhaps, centring on the woman standing in
the middle, in a long, crimson velvet dress. To understand
as well as enjoy this picture we need to know how it came
about. In 1970 Phillips acquired a postcard showing the
interior of the Mappin Art Gallery in Sheffield. Done from a
black-and-white photograph of around 1900, the coloured
postcard showed the walls of the gallery close-hung with
pictures, some of them obscured by columns and by a
sculpture in the middle of the room, some by the oblique
angle of some of the walls, and all of them distorted by their
minute size as reproduced, by coarse printing and by the
arbitrary addition of colours. Phillips decided to attempt to
reconstruct those images of which the postcard gave any
usable evidence: twenty-two pictures in all. Here is his
second version of the one he listed as No.6.

The project took some years, during which, by luck and
by research, Phillips was able to identify a few of the
originals. No.6 turned out to be *The Flag of Truce* by John
Pettie, showing soldiers bearing a white flag, at the entrance
to a castle. No garden, no idle, elegant figures, no crimson
velvet. Phillips' exercise in archaeology and interpretation
makes one wonder how interchangeable the signals we get
from pictures are, and how much our reading of them
depends on personal preferences and expectations. Did
Phillips want to see those figures and trees? Or, perhaps,
has he caused me to read them into his suggestive but
unspecific composition, exhibiting my own inclinations?
His project hints at deep curiosity and an artist's wish to
possess the whole world of art. He has written, 'my
passions are for structures, connections, correspondence,
and systems which link the sensual, visual and intellectual
worlds'. His use of existing works of arts, via the postcard in
this instance, contrasts with Redfern's [No.51]; his enquiry
into how the arts address us and what they can speak of,
invites comparison with Hamilton's thoughtful methods
and imagery [No.25].

No. 50
Conjectured Picture, Mappin Art Gallery,
Sheffield, No. 6
1976, acrylic on canvas
170 x 142 cm
Tom Phillips (copyright DACS)
photograph: Rodney Todd-White

David Redfern
Work

In 1863 the Pre-Raphaelite painter Ford Madox Brown
completed *Work*, a pictorial compendium of all classes of
people, from the idle rich to labourers and those too base to
be thought worthy of work. We can recognize in it a
particular site in north-west London and two admired
gentlemen, who are considering the scene: the writer
Thomas Carlyle, historian and social critic, and the
Reverend F D Maurice, founder of the Christian Socialist
Party. In 1977 David Redfern painted his version of the
scene, re-staging Brown's now very popular painting. He
found that the site had not changed a great deal. He used
fewer figures, and a machine to replace some of the
labourers. Carlyle and Maurice are replaced by Vic Feather,
the trade union leader known also for his support of the
arts. The old lady, a common sight in south London, and a
young woman from a fashion magazine replace Brown's
throng, whilst other people sit in their cars in a traffic jam.

The meaning of Redfern's painting, I suggest, is found
more in its general character than in the detail. Brown's
picture bustles with figures and events; Redfern's is sparse
and without charm. Brown's intention was to remind
viewers of the dignity of work, physical and intellectual.
Redfern portrays a world in which the machine has
minimized physical action and where trees are cut back
crudely to save expense. Significantly, the labourers and
their work are cut off from passers-by, just as the people
sitting in their cars are cut off from the world and each
other. What has been done to the tree has been done to
society. Carlyle's message was that money must not be
allowed to dominate society. Redfern's is that it does, and
that we are the poorer for it.

Ford Madox Brown,
Work,
1852, 1856 – 63, oil on canvas,
Manchester City Art Galleries

126

No. 51
Work
1977, oil on canvas
87.2 x 121.8 cm
Southampton City Art Gallery
photograph: Rodney Todd-White

Paula Rego
Untitled ('Girl and Dog' series)

Rego is an outstanding pictorial story-teller. She used to entertain us with pictures crowded with figures, animals and odd events. Her mind seemed a cornucopia of images and actions remembered from fairy-tales, from music-hall performances and also from the world of films and film-making, and she spilled it out with energy and with extraordinary graphic skills, leaving us in some doubt whether or not there was a message inside the evident humour. Her recent paintings use a different scale and are weightier.

In each scene of the series represented here, there is one girl and one dog and she is doing something to it: she feeds it, shaves its chin, puts it in a child's high chair or, here, fastens a chain around its neck. The girl is always purpose-ful and unrelenting, the dog compliant and miserable. Sometimes there is an observer: an owl, another bird, here part of an elephant (we say an elephant never forgets). Obviously the action is symbolic, though we may not feel sure how to evaluate it, especially in a context of feminism. Paula Rego seems to be speaking of women's power to oppress and demean through what might be mistaken for affectionate domestic play. The girl wears on her arm the spiky dog-collar which the dog should wear to protect itself against other dogs; nothing protects it against the attentions of his young mistress. She belongs to another decade, judging by her hair and dress, but her domineering manner is timeless. The ball, the box on which she sits, above all the suggestion of a round arena, imply a circus setting, yet we sense also enclosure. There is no way out.

No. 52
Untitled ('Girl and Dog' series)
1986, acrylic paint on paper
112 x 76 cm
The British Council
photograph: Rodney Todd-White

Ceri Richards
Two Musicians

    Music mattered greatly to this Welsh painter and his
family. Many of his paintings refer to music, to specific
compositions sometimes, and his art was often close to
abstraction, in search of music's sensory communication.
In this painting almost everything flows, like music. He
offers us a light, harmonious pattern of colour areas and
descriptive silhouettes. Intervals are as important as
accents, the movement of the brush as significant as the
object it is describing in its summary but loving manner.
We therefore sense the painter's presence before the scene,
his making of this vivid account of the two girls, one
playing a violin, the other seated at a piano. He omits a
great deal of information – the face of the girl on the right,
for instance – whilst stressing the curves that make up
their bodies and actions. Generally this is a flat image,
giving priority to decorative coherence, so that we are
thrilled to find the neck of the violin thrust so firmly
towards us in its centre. This and other paintings of
Richards' demonstrate his allegiance to the great French
master of modern decorative art, Matisse; elsewhere, he
demonstrated his interest also in Surrealism and in the
quirkier aspects of Cubism. Altogether, Richards took
confident possession of European modernism with an
appetite and firm grasp few British artists around him ever
achieved.

No. 53
Two Musicians
c. 1954, oil on canvas
51 x 61 cm
Arts Council Collection.
South Bank Centre, London
photograph: Eileen Tweedy Photography

William Roberts
Rush Hour

This painting by Roberts is a characteristically contradictory affair. It represents people and buses in a London street at a very busy time. There are three typical London Transport double-decker buses, painted the traditional red, and there are people of all sorts getting on and off and generally battling fairly amicably for survival.

All this activity is shown with great clarity. One bus is going to Waterloo Station; the other is off to Tooting Bec, in south London. We can distinguish each figure perfectly clearly too, as well as their various possessions. A third bus together with other elements in the picture asserts space and distance, yet the effect of the whole is flat, a network of lines and directions and a compact assembly of bodily masses. These masses are modelled in tone to give a sense of volume, yet again there is little feeling of depth and none at all of real daylight.

Roberts has adapted the classical idiom of Western painting, taking a strict reading of it, for this commonplace scene. In other words, he has used an idiom associated with the great themes of art – beginning with the gods and heroes of the ancient Greeks – for a subject which is to do with the people of today going about their daily, ordinary, quite unheroic business. This can be seen as a devaluing of the idiom; it can also be seen as an ennobling of the ordinary, with Everyman (and Everywoman) getting the attention, the desire for pictorial harmony, that was once reserved for a very few. In spite of a certain stiffness in the composition and the figures – or should we say, because of it – the energy of the action portrayed comes across powerfully.

No. 54
Rush Hour
1971, oil on canvas
121.9 x 96.5 cm
Simon Keswick
photograph: The Maclean Gallery, London

Stanley Spencer
Resurrection – The Hill of Zion

The Resurrection – the return to life of all humanity, summoned by angels' trumpets announcing the end of the world, as foretold in the Bible – obsessed Spencer by its combination of a climactic element of religious dogma and an invitation to imagine the coming together of men and women and children of all sorts. In the 1940s, whilst living among and painting the shipbuilders of Port Glasgow in Scotland, he conceived the project of honouring the place and its people in a great composite work of several canvases picturing the Resurrection in local and contemporary terms – just as at other times he pictured biblical subjects in terms of his native Cookham, as in *The Marriage at Cana* [No.56]. A cemetery on a domed hill amid redbrick houses became his location for Christ's return to earth to call and judge mankind. We see Christ among trumpet-blowing and recording angels, disciples and prophets, whilst, right and left beyond the slopes of the hill, people are rising from their graves and coming forward. Exceptionally pale, the painting as a whole announces its unreality, its non-being in a physical sense; at the same time it contains some of Spencer's most powerful figures, notably that of Christ and the disciples seated below him. The composition, too, has a dramatic force not always found in Spencer's narrative scenes, partly because of his habit of adding more and more figures to his main theme for narrative fullness. But even here, he does not deny his love of detail: witness his fond portrayal of the leaves and blossom of lilac and of other plants on the hill, and his account of the patterns of clothing and of wings.

No. 55
Resurrection – The Hill of Zion
1946, oil on canvas
109.2 x 205.7 cm
Harris Museum and Art Gallery, Preston,
Lancashire
photograph: courtesy of the Harris Museum
and Art Gallery, Preston

Stanley Spencer
The Marriage at Cana: Bride and Bridegroom

'I paint what I know', he wrote. This little picture does not advertise its basis in a religious text except through its title. What we see could be any couple of the 1920s and 1930s sitting down with family and friends to celebrate their wedding. We seem to be looking down on them a little from above: a snapshot taken by someone standing on a chair perhaps, or a moment from a film, one of those Ealing comedies, lively films with strong social sympathies, made in Britain after 1945. There was something nostalgic about them too. The painter is here recalling his first marriage: we see him and his bride of 1925 sitting down, she making that lovable but ungainly gesture with which a woman smoothes her skirt behind her. So this is autobiography, a kind of self-portrait. But it is also much more. It treats a biblical subject, itself full of symbolical meaning. We know that it was intended to be part of a sequence of pictures narrating the whole story of the Marriage at Cana, and this sequence was intended by Spencer to go with other scenes into a sort of chapel he wished to see built in his native Cookham. Inevitably, perhaps, he had to sell his work when patrons asked for it and it was dispersed, so that we have never been able to study these pictures brought together in the quasi-religious context he wanted for them. We still find it odd to see an event of about AD 30 represented in commonplace modern terms, because the nineteenth century demanded historical accuracy. But the Italian painters of the pre-Renaissance and Renaissance period told their religious stories as contemporary events, set into their own times, and it is from them that Spencer conceived the idea of creating not separate pictures but visually and intellectually coherent pictorial schemes.

No. 56
The Marriage at Cana: Bride and Bridegroom
1953, oil on canvas
60 x 50.8 cm
Glynn Vivian Art Gallery, Leisure Services
Department, Swansea City Council
photograph: courtesy of Glynn Vivian Art
Gallery

Peter Unsworth
Work in Progress

Is this a British habit or one peculiar to all human
beings? We see three figures, two men and one woman,
peering through little openings in a timber hoarding. 'Work
in progress', says the title, but we cannot see that work, only
the hoarding and the tall trees that rise portentously above
it. The theme is human curiosity, and more particularly the
pleasure we take in seeing others at work, even though the
work itself may be quite unremarkable. Here, perhaps, men
are clearing a site and digging into it to lay the foundations
of a building. The fact is that we shall never know, so the
picture addresses both the fascination of those three
persons shown in it and our own curiosity in wanting to
know what they are watching. The fact that we cannot cross
over the road to join them, picking an aperture at the right
level for our height, imparts a sense of loneliness. Similarly,
the isolation of those little openings in the hoarding keeps
the viewers in the picture apart. We share the virtue, or
vice, of curiosity, and may see it as a convivial tendency, yet
in pursuit of it we isolate ourselves. All looking at art is at
least partly a voyeuristic activity. Unsworth's scene, sharply
lit from the left by an afternoon sun and empty of detail
apart from the foliage, gives us a sense of dreamlike stillness that further distances us from any experience of work,
let alone of the kind of hubbub that we might normally
expect to find behind that hoarding.

No. 57
Work in Progress
1985, oil on canvas
130 x 97 cm
Piccadilly Gallery, London W1
photograph: Rodney Todd-White

Michael Upton
Library (The Unemployed) II
Society Restaurant I

Here are two very small paintings, forming a pair. The size of a painting determines our first response to it. A very large painting suggests public oratory; on occasion, as with Eileen Cooper's *Gift* [No.23], it can also seem to envelop us in its romantic world. Upton's pictures require our attention without demanding it, and soon reveal themselves as powerful images dealing with the important and widely relevant theme of social inequality.

He often works in series. These two images were paired by him though they come from different series. The two compositions are themselves quite distinct: the restaurant and its clients are seen from a natural eye-level, as though we were there too, while the reading room is seen from above, giving us a clear record of the space and of the objects and people in it. It looks as though all the seats in it are occupied. In the restaurant we see those able to enjoy expensive pleasures; in the public library are the unemployed, come to sit and benefit from the heating system and to read in peace if they wish. Such juxtaposing of contrasting images for didactic purposes must be a very old device, certainly known to medieval art, probably always used in didactic speech. In this sense Upton is attaching himself to a well-known method of persuasion. What is surprising about his pictures is the delicacy and the unassertive decency with which he makes his point. Stylistically they have their roots in the controlled naturalistic painting of Degas and his English disciple, Sickert. They exhibit close observation of particular places and of how people act in them; at the same time they show a constructive urge that moulds this visual information into harmonious compositions. The images are generalized, and yet they feel quite particular, and the subdued colours and tones invite our eyes to gaze calmly on both scenes.

No. 58
Library (The Unemployed) II
1985, oil on board
16.8 x 36.2 cm
courtesy Anne Berthoud Gallery, London
photograph: courtesy Anne Berthoud
Gallery Ltd

No. 59
Society Restaurant I
1986, oil on board
15.6 x 31.1 cm
courtesy Anne Berthoud Gallery, London
photograph: courtesy Anne Berthoud
Gallery Ltd

Keith Vaughan
Water, Trees and Figures II

Keith Vaughan achieved something quite rare in British painting but close to the heart of the European tradition: monumental figure images of a generalized kind, often in summary landscape settings and conveying a sense of humanity in harmony with nature. The theme goes back to ancient Greece; it became a conscious concern of modern art with Cézanne's famous figure paintings of around 1900. The issue is not size – the Cézannes are relatively large, the Vaughan is quite small – but scale: the scale of the figures in relation to the canvas area and other things represented in it, and above all the scale of the forms that constitute the image. Taking some formal ideas from Cubism (which in part developed out of Cézanne but ignored this culminating feature of his work), probably via Matisse, Vaughan constructed his figures as hard and soft, geometrical and organic. They are frontal, they are nude, they lack almost all detail and give little insight into individual personality or even sexual life. Their faces, especially that on the right, are without character. Their poses are effective as form but have no narrative role. They are not quite idealized presences but give a sense of commonplace man viewed with respect. Vaughan spoke of them as spiritual beings, and said that 'It is not to find out what makes things differ which interests me, but what unites things'. This is the basic classical impulse, here expressed with rare concision. The forms of the men are also the forms of the landscape, and Vaughan's colour chords reinforce this congruity.

No. 60
Water, Trees and Figures II
1948 – 59, oil on canvas
62.5 x 83.7 cm
The British Council
photograph: The British Council

Carel Weight
For Children: The Witches are Here

Like Stanley Spencer, whose work he admires, Carel
Weight is a pictorial story-teller. He too sometimes takes his
subjects from the Bible but more often they are at once
ordinary and imaginary, speaking of familiar human experiences in ways that reach beneath their merely visual
aspects. He is a poet of the everyday. The word 'poet' is
important here because he is not a realist: he creates
through his art images that, for all the realism of their
setting and the ordinariness of the details, deliver something quite visionary, poignant.

The setting of *For Children...* is a south London street.
The figures strike one as familiar, so the scene as a whole is
entirely persuasive. Weight's way of presenting it is firmly
descriptive, aptly showing the awkward movements of
people taken by surprise, as well as all sorts of details in the
houses and the street that make us feel well informed. He is
more interested than Spencer in the communicative power
of colour and the texture of paint. Like Spencer, he stands
in a North European tradition that goes back to Breughel in
the sixteenth century and to images in manuscripts before
that. One also senses in his work, unlike Spencer's, some
influence from photography and especially films in his
chosen viewpoint, the vivid informality of the composition
and the strong sense he gives us of the events of a particular
moment. The witches that come riding through the air on
their brooms, identified by their black clothes and pointed
hats, are familiar too, but familiar from fairy-tales rather
than from the south London streets. They are macabre,
frightening creatures, especially to children whom, it is
reported, they wish to devour. Are children still frightened
by talk of witches? Perhaps not. But the underlying theme
of such symbolic images is death and – if the fairy-tale has
a happy ending – the beginnings of a better, safe existence.
Such themes, universal to all humanity, will go on finding
poetic forms of expression.

Artists

Craigie Aitchison b.1926

David Gwinnutt

The subject matter through which Craigie
Aitchison elects to express himself is that of the
traditional artist: portrait, landscape, still life
and some religious subjects, mostly cruci-
fixions. His approach to painting is restrained,
highly calculated and precise. He uses thin
washes of paint, but with colour so sensual and
pulsating that it harnesses what could be
considered an academic art and lifts it onto an
altogether more spiritual plane.

Craigie Aitchison was born in Scotland in
1926, and studied at the Slade School of Fine
Art in London from 1952 to 1954. He then won
an Italian government scholarship which
enabled him to travel and work in Italy and later
to visit museums and galleries in many parts of
Europe. He has been awarded a number of
prizes for painting and in 1978 was elected
Associate of the Royal Academy (ARA). Craigie
Aitchison has exhibited widely in Britain and
abroad, and his work is represented in all of the
major public collections in the United Kingdom.

Frank Auerbach b.1931

A rich texture of thickly applied paint has characterized Auerbach's work since he was a student at the Royal College of Art in the early 1950s. The range of his palette has evolved from monochrome black and white and earth colours to a broader, brighter spectrum in recent years. His subject matter has remained constant: building sites, views from Primrose Hill in London and portraits of very close friends.

Frank Auerbach was born in Berlin in 1931 and was sent to England in 1939; he never saw members of his immediate family again. Auerbach studied art at Hampstead Garden Suburb Institute and Borough Polytechnic, where he was taught by David Bomberg. He gained a silver medal and first-class honours at St Martin's School of Art, where he was a student from 1948 to 1952, before studying at the Royal College of Art from 1952 to 1958. In 1986 he represented Britain at the Venice Biennale where he was awarded the *Lion d'Or*.

John Bellany b.1942

John Bellany is a highly individual artist, and has always appeared to be independent of any group or movement or fashion. His imagery is based on the life of the fishing village of Port Seton on the estuary of the Firth of Forth, where he was born and brought up. He has, however, spent most of his professional working life in London. He paints in an expressionist style, and reveals a debt to Van Gogh, Ensor and Beckmann. In recent years his touch has lightened, but the fish, birds, fishermen and the sea remain.

In 1988 Bellany became very seriously ill and spent a long period in hospital. He fought for his life by turning his hospital room into a studio and painting, from his bed, a series of works of himself and of the doctors and nurses, as an antidote to pain.

Born in Port Seton, Scotland in 1942, John Bellany studied at Edinburgh College of Art from 1960 to 1965. He won a postgraduate travelling scholarship to the Netherlands and Belgium in 1965, and then studied at the Royal College of Art in London from 1965 to 1968. In 1986 he was elected Associate of the Royal Academy (ARA). He has exhibited frequently and widely since 1963, and his work is represented in major British public collections.

Tony Bevan b.1951

Tony Bevan's paintings of people convey an outward manifestation of an inward state. A state that might be psychological, sociological, emotional... They refer, through metaphor, to literary sources, and to contemporary British life, frequently brutal. They are tough and uncompromising, revealing a remarkable insight into the human state in the late 1980s. The people through whom he conveys his message are not models in the traditional sense, but are specific images of certain human types, isolated, as in an icon, with no reference to location. Surface is important to his paintings: a rich, gritty texture is often used to emphasize his point of view.

Tony Bevan was born in 1951 in Bradford, an industrial town in the south of Yorkshire with a high population of immigrants from Asia. He studied at Bradford College of Art from 1968 to 1971 and subsequently at Goldsmiths' School of Art and Design in London from 1971 to 1974 and the Slade School of Fine Art from 1974 to 1976. He has exhibited his work regularly since 1970. In 1987-88 the Institute of Contemporary Art in London organized a major exhibition of his work, *Painting from the Inside Out*, which toured in Britain.

Otto Schneider

Peter Blake RA b.1932

Peter Blake has been hailed as the father of Pop art in Britain. His paintings are careful and realistic. In his earlier work he employed collage and assemblage, using objects from his large collection of mementoes, postcards and badges, all objects of popular culture. He was a pioneer in this whilst still a student at the Royal College of Art in the mid-1950s.

In 1975 he founded, with others, the Brotherhood of Ruralists, an association of painters who, on a nineteenth-century model, grouped together to work in the countryside.

Peter Blake was born in 1932. He studied at Gravesend School of Art from 1946 to 1951 and at the Royal College of Art from 1953 to 1956. He was elected Associate of the Royal Academy (ARA) in 1974, and became full Royal Academician (RA) in 1981.

William Bowyer RA b.1926

William Bowyer was born in Leek in
Staffordshire in 1926. He studied at Berslem
School of Art, Stoke-on-Trent and at the Royal
College of Art, graduating in 1949. His teaching
career, in Gravesend School of Art, Maidstone
College of Art, the Central School in London
and Walthamstow School of Art, culminated in
his becoming Head of Fine Art at Maidstone
from 1971 to 1981.

Bowyer was elected Associate of the Royal
Academy (ARA) in 1973 and Royal Academician
(RA) in 1981. He is a member of The Royal
Society of Painters in Water Colours and The
Royal Society of Portrait Painters. He is also
Honorary Secretary of the New English Art
Club. William Bowyer has exhibited widely and
his paintings are in many private and public
collections, notably the Arts Council, The
National Portrait Gallery and the Marylebone
Cricket Club (MCC) Museum, Lords. The suc-
cess of his portrait of Viv Richards may, in part,
result from William Bowyer's keen interest in
the sport of cricket.

Boyd and Evans
Fionnuala Boyd b.1944
Leslie Evans b.1945

Boyd and Evans: two artists working as one. In order to disguise their individual 'hand-writing' in these jointly produced paintings, Boyd and Evans used a spray-gun to deliver highly (photo) realistic images. They discuss content and image exhaustively before working on a canvas, and are united in their intellectual approach, which has an affinity with surrealism – the juxtaposition of unrelated images forging a new idea. In recent work they have used their spray techniques less often, introducing freer brushwork, which, through their drawings, has become so alike as to be indistinguishable.

Fionnuala Boyd was born in 1944 and studied at Leeds University. Leslie Evans, born in 1945, studied at Leeds College of Art. They began working together in 1968. Boyd and Evans have exhibited widely since the early 1970s, both in Britain and internationally, and their works are represented in major public collections.

Paul Brason b.1952

In the early stages of his career Paul Brason worked as a designer and scenic artist for the Haymarket Theatre in Leicester, and for Richmond Theatre Productions and the Ballet Rambert in London. He also worked with Editions Alecto on two publishing projects: *A Voyage Round Great Britain*, a co-publication with the Tate Gallery, in 1977; and as Editor of *'Banks' Florilegium*, a co-publication between Egreton-Williams Studio, Alecto Historical Editions and the British Museum of Natural History in 1979.

At the same time Paul Brason continued to paint and exhibit his work; in 1978 he began working on large figure paintings. Since 1980 he has exhibited regularly in the National Portrait Gallery's annual Portrait Award Exhibitions, being awarded a prize in 1983. These exhibitions brought with them the commissions which have enabled Brason to paint full time. His commissioned work includes portraits of Mrs Margaret Thatcher and HRH Prince Michael of Kent.

Born in 1952, Paul Brason studied at Hastings School of Art in 1968 and at Camberwell College of Art in London from 1969 to 1972.

Jeffery Camp RA b.1923

People in places with dramatic perspectives, figures on top of cliffs or floating over the Thames – the contrast between intimate relationships and the wide open spaces in which the figures are dropped features time and again in Jeffery Camp's canvases. His paintings, carefully constructed but with free and sensual use of paint, are celebrations of life.

Jeffery Camp was born in Lowestoft in Suffolk in 1923. He studied at both Lowestoft and Ipswich School of Art, and from 1941 to 1944 attended Edinburgh College of Art, where he was taught by William Gillies and John Maxwell. Jeffery Camp was elected Royal Academician (RA) in 1984.

Sir William Coldstream Kt.CBE
1908-1987

William Coldstream developed in his art a degree of objectivity and sustained observation, together with a restrained use of paint, that influenced many of his peers and, eventually, his students. His desire for accuracy is epitomized in his statement of 1937: 'As far as I can remember once I have started painting I am occupied mainly with putting things in the right place.' Coldstream's choice of subject matter – portraits, places and still lifes – was also consistent throughout his career.

William Coldstream was born in 1908 in Northumberland. He studied at the Slade School of Fine Art from 1926 to 1929 under Professor Tonks. In 1938 he founded the Euston Road School of Painting with Victor Pasmore, Rodrigo Moynihan and Claude Rogers, having abandoned painting for film-making for a period of about three years.

Coldstream was appointed Slade Professor in 1948 and elected Fellow of University College, London in 1953. During his time at the Slade (he retired in 1975) he developed the School into a centre of excellence. In the period 1958 to 1971 he did much to reshape the national pattern of art education through his innovative 'Coldstream reports' for the national advisory committee on art education.

William Coldstream was awarded the CBE in 1952 and, four years later, was appointed to the rank of Knight Bachelor. He died in 1987.

Eileen Cooper b.1953

Courtesy Benjamin Rhodes Gallery, London

Eileen Cooper's approach to her painting is completely natural and spontaneous. She does not pre-plan a work, but just begins, releasing the mood of the moment. The paintings are as much celebrations of events in her own life as they are statements about maternity and rearing children. She expresses herself intuitively, using strong and luscious colours with bold brushstrokes, influenced by Gauguin and the German Expressionists.

Born in 1953, Eileen Cooper studied at Goldsmiths' College in London from 1971 to 1974, and subsequently at the Royal College of Art until 1977. She has exhibited regularly in London since the late 1970s; her work has also been included in a number of group exhibitions internationally.

P J Crook b.1945

The paintings of P J Crook show a world of
foreboding, silence and intrigue, spiced with a
heavy post-Freudian symbolism. They reveal the
influence of the surrealist painters Balthus,
de Chirico and Delvaux. Her palette ranges from
strong, contrasting colours to sombre grey and
brown monochromes. To emphasize the feelings
of mystery and spatial ambiguity of her paintings, P J Crook has employed the technique of
continuing her painting over its own frame, as
well as painting on surfaces which are in relief.

Born in 1945, P J Crook has lived in
Gloucestershire, the Hebrides and London. She
studied at Gloucestershire College of Art from
1960 to 1965, specializing in textiles and printmaking, in order to acquire marketable skills.
She has exhibited regularly both at the Portal
Gallery in London and in many group exhibitions. Her work is particularly popular in
America.

Ken Currie b.1960

Ken Currie's observations on the human condition in a city where many are socially underprivileged, are imbued with optimism. The working-class ethic of self-improvement appears alongside the rewards of a night out on the town after a week of industrial labour. Currie's realism is full of movement and energy, his dark palette shot through with a vitality that is echoed in the bright, shining light of the haloes with which he frequently surrounds his figures. '... [My] aim, in the end, is to paint about the realities of the human condition as well as to depict the existing possibilities for world reconstruction.'

Born in 1960 in North Shields, Northumberland, of Scottish parents, Currie studied social science at Paisley College of Technology from 1977 to 1978 and attended Glasgow School of Art from 1978 to 1983. He has exhibited widely since 1980 and his work is represented in many important public collections.

Joan Dawson b.1958

Joan Dawson's paintings are carefully crafted. In the early 1980s her concerns were based in social realism, which remains a continuing interest. Of her work she writes that, 'it would, I hope, be accessible to the people I actually paint about'.

Born in 1958, Joan Dawson studied fine art at the University of Leeds from 1977 to 1982, graduating with a first-class honours degree. She has exhibited widely since 1982 and has received a number of awards, including West Midlands Arts Artist-in-Industry at Hardy Spicer Ltd in Birmingham, a Residency at the Walker Art Gallery in Liverpool, and a West Midlands Arts Residency at Stuart Crystal in Stourbridge.

Mark Fairnington b.1957

Mark Fairnington lives in a high-rise block of flats on a council estate in south-east London, and his paintings are based on what he sees of urban life around him. 'I use a narrative style that tells the stories of everyday events – break-ins, domestic strife, fire, officialdom, furniture dumping, dogs and more dogs. To me these are contemporary folk tales, a sort of urban mythology.' His more recent work, however, is tending towards a simplification of the human form, with references to historical paintings that interest him. He has also made some 'light box' paintings which suggest that his earlier studies in sculpture are surfacing now.

Born in 1957, Mark Fairnington studied at Canterbury College of Art from 1975 to 1976, and at St Martin's School of Art from 1976 to 1980, where he gained a BA in sculpture. He is currently attending an MA course, part-time, at Goldsmiths' College of Art.

Amanda Faulkner b.1953

David Oldfield

Amanda Faulkner's paintings, drawings and prints raise both issues and questions – on human interaction, power, submission – all related to feminism. She questions the structures of our lives and how we see ourselves, through images such as mother and child, women, and the things that surround their lives. Some works contain mythological and historical references. Painted with spontaneous, almost expressionistic vigour, her work has gradually evolved from something deeply personal and introverted, cloaked in formal abstraction, through intensely complex compositions full of movement, towards a calmer, more celebratory and more optimistic art.

Born in Dorset in 1953, Amanda Faulkner studied at Bournemouth College of Art from 1978 to 1979, at Ravensbourne College of Art from 1979 to 1982 (specializing in fine art), and at Chelsea School of Art from 1982 to 1983, where she took her MA in printmaking.

Rose Garrard b.1946

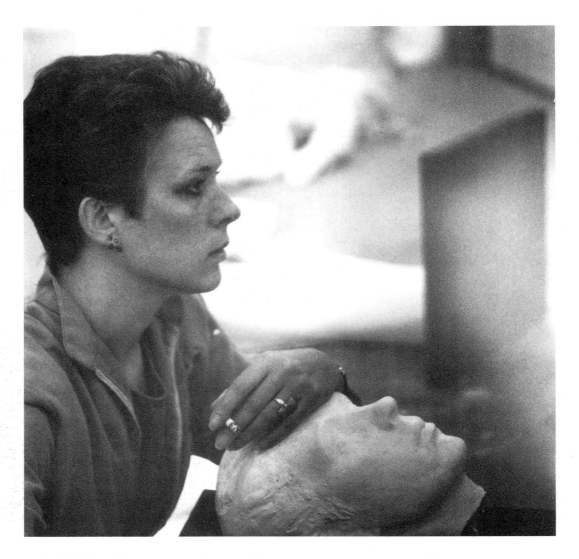

In 1984 Rose Garrard wrote of her art, 'The work is a way of exploring, questioning, discovering, and extending my awareness of the restrictions affecting who I can be. I hope that it can engender a similar response in others. I believe that this *live process* is as central to Art as it is to Feminism. Both are integral to my practice as an artist, each part of discovering the other.' Whilst her work has developed since then, the basic principles revealed in her statement still apply. Rose Garrard trained as a sculptor, and uses sculptural techniques to further ends, employing a wide variety of media including clothes and television. She has a continuing interest in history, particularly that of womens' issues, and this recurs constantly in her strong and deeply felt imagery.

Born in 1946 in Bewdley in Worcestershire, Rose Garrard studied at Stourbridge College of Art, Worcestershire from 1965 to 1966, at Birmingham College of Art from 1966 to 1969, and at Chelsea School of Art from 1969 to 1970. She has exhibited regularly since 1967.

Patrick George b.1923

Patrick George had decided that he would be a painter by the time he was thirteen years old. Together with Lucian Freud he set up an oil painting club at Bryanston, the public school where they were both educated. His subjects have been the people and places close to him: models and friends in London, his studio, views from his window, and the landscape of Suffolk where he has a cottage and where he paints in the open air. His paintings are realistic and carefully measured, a trait he shares with Coldstream, whom he knew at the Slade.

Patrick George was born in Manchester in 1923. He studied at Edinburgh College of Art and at Camberwell School of Art in London. In 1949 he joined the staff of the Slade School of Fine Art, to which he returned after a period of teaching at the Nigerian College of Art and Technology, Zaria, in 1959. Between the years 1985 and 1987 he was Slade Professor at University College, London.

Work by Patrick George can be found in public collections throughout Britain; he has exhibited regularly since the early 1940s.

Anthony Green RA b.1939

courtesy Mayor Rowan Gallery

Anthony Green's paintings concentrate minutely on his wife Mary and on people, places and occasions, all remembered with wit and presented with intense vision. Since the 1960s he has worked on a large scale with great attention to detail and the perspective flattened out to resemble the image seen through a fish-eye lens. His canvases are often eccentrically shaped, accentuating his frequently bizarre narratives.

Born in London in 1939, Anthony Green studied at the Slade School of Fine Art from 1956 to 1960. In 1960 he won a French government scholarship and, in 1967, a United States fellowship that spanned two years. Anthony Green was elected Associate of the Royal Academy (ARA) in 1971 and Royal Academician (RA) in 1977. He has exhibited regularly in London since 1977 and is well known internationally.

Peter Griffin b.1947

When Peter Griffin was a student at the Royal College of Art he painted coal-mines and miners familiar to him from his native Yorkshire in the north of England.

His imagery was enriched by his gradual discovery of some of the giants of twentieth-century art, for example Matta, L'Hote and Braque. Two years at the British School in Rome, 1977 to 1979, had a further profound effect on his development as an artist.

Born in 1947, in Wakefield, Yorkshire, Peter Griffin studied at Wakefield School of Art from 1970 to 1971, at Loughborough College of Art from 1971 to 1974, and at the Royal College of Art, London from 1974 to 1977. He was awarded the Rome Scholarship for painting in 1977.

Peter Griffin has exhibited his work regularly in Britain and Italy from 1974, and his work is in collections in Britain, France, Italy, Australia and the United States.

Maggi Hambling b.1945

Maggi Hambling is a portrait painter of great intelligence and perception. She researches her subjects thoroughly and creates paintings that tell us much about the life of the sitter. She shares with the painter Francis Bacon an appreciation of the sensual qualities in paint and a need for subjects to be expressed with urgency. This can be seen in her water-colours depicting sunset and sunrise and, equally, in her extraordinarily vivid drawings of bulls.

Maggi Hambling was born in Suffolk in 1945. She studied with Lett Harris and Cedric Morris from 1960 onwards and was a student at Ipswich School of Art from 1962 to 1964, at Camberwell School of Art from 1964 to 1967 and at the Slade School of Fine Art from 1967 to 1969. In 1969 she received the Boise Travel Award, New York, and in 1977 won an Arts Council award. Maggi Hambling was the first Artist-in-Residence at the National Gallery in London, from 1980 to 1981. She has exhibited widely since 1967 and her work is represented in many public collections.

Richard Hamilton b.1922

Early in his career, Hamilton produced paintings concerned with the qualities inherent in mass media, at the same time delivering his well-known characterization of Pop art: 'Popular; Transient; Expendable; Low Cost; Mass Produced; Young; Witty; Sexy; Gimmicky; Glamorous; Big Business'. He has remained interested in print as a vehicle for his ideas, which, with his paintings, explore themes in literature and politics.

Richard Hamilton was born in 1922 in London. He worked for a year in advertising in 1936, at the same time attending evening classes at Westminster Technical College and at St Martin's School of Art. From 1938 to 1940 he studied painting at the Royal Academy Schools, resuming his studies there in 1946. He studied painting at the Slade School of Fine Art from 1948 to 1951. Richard Hamilton's work has been widely acclaimed internationally; he has had numerous exhibitions and his work is represented in collections in Britain and abroad.

Patrick Heron CBE b.1920

Bob Berry, Art-on-Film

Patrick Heron is known for his large colour-saturated abstract canvases, featuring interlocking shapes which in the 1960s were free-formed and revealed the brushwork, in the 1970s were tighter and hard-edged with dynamic juxtapositions of pure flat colour, and in the 1980s were dappled and luxuriously textured, reminiscent of the beautiful garden at Eagles Nest, his home on the western coast of the Cornish peninsula.

'The only rule I follow while painting is this: I always allow my hand to surprise me (the lines of all the frontiers in my recent paintings are drawn-in in a matter of a few seconds): also, I always follow impulse – for instance in the choice of colours; deliberation is fruitless. But this does not mean that every act connected with the painting of the picture is not deliberate: it is.' (Patrick Heron, *Colour in my Painting*, Studio International, December 1969.)

Born in 1920 at Headingly in Leeds, Patrick Heron was a part-time student at the Slade School of Fine Art from 1937 to 1939. For most of his professional life he has lived and worked in London and Cornwall; he has a fine reputation both as artist and as a perceptive writer on art. (He is author of an impressive list of books and articles.) He has received many honours: in 1977 he was awarded a CBE and more recently in 1987 an Honorary Doctorate (RCA). Patrick Heron has exhibited his work widely since the 1940s and his work is well known internationally.

Susan Hiller b.1942

Susan Hiller's work defies rigid definition. It does not fit the readily available categories liked by the tidy historian. She uses a multiplicity of materials as vehicles for her ideas, including photography, film, video, calligraphy, and paint in both wall works and installations. Hiller investigates through her work the issues in our culture and questions her own stance within it. 'A woman is mute within our culture in that when she speaks, she speaks as a man.' (*Time Out*, 8-12 November 1986.)

Susan Hiller was born in 1942 in the United States, where she studied at Smith College (BA 1961) and Tulane University (MA 1965). After anthropological field work in Central America she moved to Europe at the end of the 1960s, living mainly in France and England with long periods of travel in North Africa, India and the Far East. She lives and works in London, and her work is well known internationally.

David Hockney b.1937

Jerry Sohn

David Hockney achieved his first taste of
fame whilst still a student at the Royal College
of Art. His witty and sometimes outrageous
personality fuelled the publicity that he
enjoyed. His work at this stage was inspired by
Dubuffet and Walt Whitman and was
deliberately naïve in imagery and technique. In
1964 he went to live in Los Angeles, a move
which had a profound effect on his palette. The
light and colour in the Californian landscape
and a hedonistic life-style are reflected in his
swimming-pool paintings and portraits of
friends. From 1973 to 1975 Hockney lived in
Paris, where his interest began to turn towards
Cubism and Picasso. His analysis of form and
space, and the decorative, textured surfaces of
recent Californian paintings, reveal this interest.
This 'Cubist' approach can also be seen in the
photographic collages which he has made since
1982.

David Hockney is an outstanding draughtsman, print-maker and stage designer; he has
recently experimented in drawing with light,
using computer technology.

Born in 1937 in Bradford, Yorkshire,
Hockney studied at Bradford School of Art from
1953 to 1957, and at the Royal College of Art
from 1959 to 1963 (Gold Medal). In 1985 he was
elected Associate of the Royal Academy (ARA);
he has been awarded a number of honorary
degrees by British and American universities.
His work has been exhibited widely and is
represented in collections all over the world.
His most recent retrospective exhibition, organized by the Los Angeles County Museum of Art,
was shown at the Tate Gallery in London from
October 1988 to January 1989.

Peter Howson b.1958

New relationships between contemporary life and contemporary art are constantly sought by artists, and Peter Howson has found much in the Glasgow of the 1980s to fuel his passion. His works depict a masculine world of soldiers, boxers, body-builders, sportsmen, dossers and characters found 'in the streets around Howson's studio in Gallowgate, Glasgow's old hangman's quarters, [where] muttering and toothless old men pass you on the way to The Saracen Head Inn, the oldest pub in the city, built in 1775 on the site of an old leper's hospital'. (Waldemar Januszczak, 1987, in *Saracen Heads* exhibition catalogue, Angela Flowers Gallery, October 1987.)

Peter Howson was born in London in 1958. He moved to Scotland in 1962 and studied for two separate periods at Glasgow School of Art, 1975-77 and 1979-81. Between these periods of study he had a variety of jobs and travelled in Europe. Howson has been the recipient of a number of prizes for his work and is represented in public collections throughout Britain. He lives and works in Glasgow.

Andrzej Jackowski b.1947

Andrzej Jackowski's paintings have frequently been referred to as poems in paint. His work represents a reverie, an archaic imagery born of inner examination, made concrete through a poetic vocabulary inspired by poets he reveres – Rilke and Bachelard, for example.

Jackowski was brought up until the age of seven speaking only Polish, which surely reinforced in him a deep sense of his family origins. He has said, 'I feel akin to the expressive image of the Northern European painters, but as well, wanting all that sun and warmth from Tuscany, from Lorenzetti and Giotto.' He brings to us, with infinite care and skill, the painted images of his innermost searches.

Born in 1947, Andrzej Jackowski studied at Camberwell School of Art from 1966 to 1967. He was dismissed from his painting course at Falmouth School of Art, which he attended from 1967 to 1969, but, on the recommendation of Peter de Francia, studied at the Royal College of Art from 1974 to 1977. He has exhibited his work regularly since 1976 and is represented in important public collections in Britain.

Allen Jones RA b.1937

Allen Jones was a student of the Royal College of Art at the same time as R B Kitaj, David Hockney, Peter Blake and others who were at the forefront of the Pop art movement in Britain. His earlier work reveals an interest in Abstract Expressionism, which he applied to figurative painting, and in the mid-1960s in New York he began to use the glossy, fetishistic imagery gleaned from commercial art which he refined to a more illusive mode of painting. His colours are vibrant, fresh and exuberant; recent free-standing figures of girls and dancing couples, cut from flat sheets of metal, are also painted in the same range.

Born in 1937 in Southampton, of Welsh parents, Jones was brought up in London. He studied at Hornsey College of Art, London from 1955 to 1959 and at the Royal College of Art from 1959 to 1960. He has taught here and abroad, and in 1988-89 he designed stage sets and costumes for the Rambert Dance Company's *Cinema*. He was elected Royal Academician (RA) in 1981. Allen Jones is internationally acclaimed, and his work is represented in major collections in Britain and abroad.

Ken Kiff b.1935

The people in Ken Kiff's paintings come from both his real world and the world of his mind. He was helped by psychoanalysis during the late 1950s and early 1960s to come to terms with his imagination, in order to release it in a meaningful and creative way, to balance the outside world with the internal.

His work now is concerned with the dynamics of painting. Colour is the primary vehicle for his images: he uses it in broad textured areas, sometimes scraping away and reapplying it. Area and mass then take precedence over line and tone. Images are strange – sometimes violent, often gentle.

Kiff was born in Essex in 1935, and entered art school at the age of twenty, studying at Hornsey School of Art from 1955 to 1961. He has exhibited regularly since the early 1970s, and his work is represented in major public collections.

Leon Kossoff b.1926

Leon Kossoff has drawn and painted London since the age of twelve. He was born in 1926 of Russian-Jewish parents, who settled in northeast London and ran a bakery in the East End. '... Bethnal Green, the City, Willesden Junction, York Way and Dalston. I have painted its bomb sites, building sites, excavations and railways ...'

His paintings are characterized by rich surfaces of heavy impasto. Thick paint and sombre colours have recently given way to a lighter, brighter palette, and the paint is applied a little less thickly. His subject matter remains highly selective, and Kossoff maintains an individual stance in the London art world, bearing no allegiance to any group or movement.

From 1949 to 1953 Kossoff studied at Borough Polytechnic, attending David Bomberg's evening classes between 1950 and 1952. From 1955 to 1956 he studied painting at the Royal College of Art. He has had solo exhibitions in London and Oxford, and his work is represented in major public collections.

Jock McFadyen b.1950

Jock McFadyen's work has evolved rapidly since the early 1980s. He studied for his BA and Master's degree in painting at Chelsea School of Art, London from 1973 to 1977. He was influenced there by figurative artists of the Pop art generation, including David Hockney and Allen Jones. His work made particular use of media-influenced imagery and included elements of caricature and the conceptual.

His style shifted during a year-long spell as Artist-in-Residence at the National Gallery towards the visual and the expressive, and his imagery began to dwell more on the private sphere.

Jock McFadyen claims that, 'I never wanted to be a jokey artist; I wanted to be serious and fast-moving'. His paintings seek to reveal the strength of the mainly working-class people that he portrays. Places are equally as important as characters: he identifies with cities like Liverpool, Belfast, New York and East Berlin, because they all have 'some kind of tension' which is re-created in his images.

Bruce McLean b.1944

As an artist Bruce McLean defies any single category. He is a sculptor, performer, print-maker, writer, film-maker, painter, and more. Ideas spill from one medium to the next. He employs satire and pun, often overlaying serious issues with glamour. To get us off guard? Painted, it seems, with a performer's zeal, his canvases are vigorous, glamorous, humorous and stylish, and reveal many layers of meaning. He may, for example, present fashionable beauty, but be dealing with underlying issues of immense seriousness. In the leaflet accompanying the exhibition *Bruce McLean Monotypes SB Factor 2-15* (Scottish Gallery, London 1989), he writes: 'These images are of beautiful people with beautiful bodies, oiling, broiling, basting, burning, bathing and blacking against beautiful backgrounds, made in a beautiful way, but dealing with issues such as erosion, pollution, and the destruction of our beautiful environment.'

Bruce McLean was born in Glasgow in 1944. He studied at Glasgow School of Art from 1961 to 1963 and at St Martin's School of Art, London from 1963 to 1966. In 1981 he was awarded a German fellowship to study in Berlin for a year. He has worked publicly since 1965 and is acclaimed in Britain, in Europe and in the United States.

Tate Gallery Liverpool (Tom Wood)

Alexander Moffat b.1943

Sean Hudson

Moffat is primarily, but not exclusively, a portrait painter. He expresses ideas in painting using the human figure. These ideas are often his own strongly-held political views, serving to convey the inner qualities of the sitter. Moffat is equally concerned with the formal problems that preoccupy a painter – composition, line, colour, form. Twentieth-century artists that have influenced Moffat include Leger, Beckmann, Munch, Kokoschka, Picasso and Matisse.

Born in 1943 in Dunfermline, Fife, Alexander Moffat studied painting at Edinburgh College of Art from 1960 to 1964. He has held appointments as visiting lecturer in Winchester and Croydon Art Schools, and at the Royal College of Art, and has been teaching in the painting studios of Glasgow School of Art since 1979. Glasgow's students, who include Ken Currie and Peter Howson, have enjoyed particular critical acclaim in recent years at a very early age. Moffat has exhibited his work in Britain, frequently in Scotland, and in Europe since 1971. His work is represented in many public collections including the Pushkin Museum, Moscow. He lives in Edinburgh.

Rodrigo Moynihan CBE RA b.1910

Moynihan studied painting at the Slade School of Fine Art from 1928 to 1931. He was an official war artist during 1943 and 1944. His early work in the 1930s was abstract, showing concern with texture. During the 1940s he developed skills as a portraitist and an interest in still life developed from the war period. He returned to abstraction in 1956 and since the 1970s has painted portraits and objects seen in the studio.

Rodrigo Moynihan was Professor of Painting at the Royal College of Art from 1948 to 1957; he was elected Associate of the Royal Academy (ARA) in 1944 and full Royal Academician (RA) in 1978. He was awarded the CBE in 1953. A retrospective exhibition of his paintings was held at the Royal Academy in 1978.

Michael Murfin b.1954

Michael Murfin was born in St Neots, Cambridgeshire in 1954, and it is the life and activities of the agricultural fenlands that provide his subject matter, as he still lives in the area. Landscape, farmers, waterways and the sea are all treated with a formal approach rooted in an appreciation and understanding of great artists from the past. Piero della Francesca, Paulo Ucello, Stubbs and Degas, all have had their effect on his vision. Poetry and music have also left their mark on his work, whether in a title or as a parallel form of composition.

Murfin studied at Leicester Polytechnic during 1972 and 1973, at Trent Polytechnic, Nottingham from 1973 to 1976 and at Birmingham Polytechnic from 1976 to 1977. He has had exhibitions regularly since 1978 and his work is represented in many important public collections in Britain.

Humphrey Ocean b.1951

Portraits, both commissioned and as observations of contemporary life, are central to Humphrey Ocean's work. Some compositions, of two or more figures, perhaps in a cityscape or in a garden, say more about relationships and convey an ambiguity which might tease our response.

His paintings are developed, sometimes through photographs, certainly through drawings and tracings which are moved, altered and drawn again. A gentle control of colour is merged into carefully undulated tonal areas, shapes are clearly designed and compositions rigorously balanced.

Humprehy Ocean was born in 1951. Between 1967 and 1973 he studied successively at Tunbridge Wells, Brighton and Canterbury School of Art. He is a bass player and in 1976 toured the USA as Artist-in-Residence with Paul McCartney's group *Wings*. He has painted commissions for the National Portrait Gallery and the Imperial War Museum.

Exhibiting frequently in group exhibitions, such as the Royal Academy's Summer Show and the National Portrait Gallery's annual John Player exhibition, Ocean has seldom had solo shows. A notable exception was an exhibition of his work at the Ferens Art Gallery in Hull, in which a group of his paintings were exhibited together with his own selection of works from the gallery's remarkable collection.

Bryan Organ b.1933

Bryan Organ is popularly known for his portraits of members of the Royal Family, including the Prince of Wales, Princess Anne and Prince Philip; they are perceptive, controversial, admired and always noted by the media, not always for reasons of artistic merit. His integrity as an artist is paramount, however, in that he searches for the truth about his sitters and gives careful consideration to composition and handling of paint. (He works primarily with acrylic paint because of its fast drying properties.) An early influence on Organ was Graham Sutherland: this shows in a somewhat freer early style, whereas his later work is more controlled, more precise. In addition to commissions, Bryan Organ paints portraits because he is interested in the sitter (the portrait of Mr and Mrs Sharples [No.13] is an example); he also chooses other subjects that he finds exciting, whether they be flowers, birds of prey, greyhounds or motorbikes. In an interview with Graham Hughes, the editor of the art magazine *Arts Review* (17 July 1987), Organ says of his portraits, 'I prefer to call them pictures of people'.

Born in 1933, Organ studied at Loughborough College of Art from 1952 to 1955 and at the Royal Academy Schools in London from 1955 to 1959. He has had regular solo exhibitions at the Redfern Gallery in London since 1967, and his work is in many public collections.

Tom Phillips b.1937

Isabelle Blondiau

Tom Phillips is an artist of great intelligence and perception. His observations, reading and reflection are as wide as the imagery he derives from them. He is meticulous in his planning and research, analysing and delving into a subject in the most rigorous way. Yet he has an abiding concern for chance procedures which enrich and vitalize his work.

He uses music and literature to create new forms visually, as well as writing his own musical compositions and diaries and making films. He makes use of found objects and images, and uses collage techniques in addition to painting, drawing and printmaking. An avid collector, Tom Phillips has a particular interest in African art.

As a portrait painter Phillips requires lengthy sittings and makes many preliminary drawings and paintings, in order to find a satisfactory rapport with his subject. Many of his portraits also include further portrayals of the sitter at other points in time, or engaged in an activity typical to him or her.

Born in London in 1937, Tom Phillips was educated at St Catherine's College, Oxford, where he studied, primarily, Anglo-Saxon literature, and at Camberwell School of Art in London, under Frank Auerbach. At Oxford he was much influenced by the art historian Edgar Wind, whose lectures on iconography and Renaissance art he attended.

He was elected Associate of the Royal Academy (ARA) in 1984, and has exhibited in numerous exhibitions in Britain and abroad. During the winter of 1989 a major exhibition of his work was held at the National Portrait Gallery in London.

David Redfern b.1947

David Redfern was born in 1947, in Burton upon Trent, Staffordshire. He studied at Reading University, Fine Art Department from 1965 to 1969, gaining a first-class honours degree. From 1969 to 1971 he studied at the Slade School of Fine Art, and from that time until 1983 he worked in London at the Arts Council's Serpentine Gallery (in Hyde Park) as the head gallery assistant, painting in his own time.

His paintings form a visual commentary on contemporary urban society, but are studies in subtlety rather than photo-realist micro-precision. They have many points of origin and references to art of the past – to artists like Piero della Francesca, Poussin and Ford Madox Brown. His urban landscapes, sometimes empty, frequently peopled, are an equivalent in paint to the real world.

Paula Rego b.1935

The Times Newspapers Ltd

Paula Rego's paintings are full of the darker sides of life and human activity. Childhood memories, stories to be told, fears and occasional feelings of comfort are all brought into her compositions.

As a student at the Slade School of Fine Art in London, Paula Rego, who had been brought up in Portugal, was forced to come to terms with her intensely personal expressions. Criticism and occasional praise from her tutors helped her to paint her world of fantasies with conviction and persuasive power. We feel, through her canvases, the reality of her personal concerns, and can find parallels with our own experiences if we search deeply enough.

Born in Lisbon in 1935, Paula Rego studied at the Slade School of Fine Art from 1957 to 1963. She has exhibited widely since 1955, and her work is represented in many public collections.

Ceri Richards CBE 1903-1971

Ida Kar

Born in 1903, Ceri Richards studied first at Swansea School of Art from 1921 to 1924 and then at the Royal College of Art from 1924 to 1927. His early work from the 1930s, when he produced painted relief constructions using wood and metal, was influenced by the surrealist art of Picasso and Ernst.

He had a lifelong love of music which is revealed in his later work; poetry, too, can be seen to be an important source. In addition to paintings, reliefs and graphic work, Richards produced a number of opera sets and costumes as well as murals and images for churches.

A contemporary of Moore and Sutherland, Richards was at the centre of the London art world for many years. He taught at the Royal College of Art from 1956 to 1961, and was created Honorary Fellow of the Royal College in 1961. He was awarded the CBE in 1960. Richards' work was exhibited widely in his lifetime, both in Britain and abroad – a major retrospective exhibition of his work was held at the Tate Galley in 1981. Ceri Richards died in 1971.

William Roberts RA 1895-1980

William Roberts was born in Hackney, London in 1895. He studied at the Slade School of Fine Art from 1910 to 1913 and then travelled extensively in France and Italy. His early subjects were religious and mythological, becoming increasingly simplified and figurative in style.

He was closely associated with Wyndham Lewis and the Vorticist group, signing the Vorticist manifesto in 1914 calling for expression of movement and activity in art. His figures became more angular and were often images of band musicians or popular dancers, using Vorticism's strident colours.

Roberts joined the army in 1916 and served in France. On his return to England two years later he became an official war artist.

In the 1920s his work softened, tonal values were carefully modulated and his palette became less strident. He continued to paint people, portraits and scenes of London life.

William Roberts was elected Associate of the Royal Academy (ARA) in 1958 and full Royal Academician (RA) in 1966. He died in London in 1980.

Self-Portrait, 1949, Tate Gallery Archive 8214.90

Leonard Rosoman OBE RA b.1913

Leonard Rosoman is particularly known for his mural paintings, which include work for the Brussels World Fair (in 1958), Lambeth College Chapel, London and the Royal Academy's restaurant.

Not normally known for portraiture, Rosoman says of that subject: 'The word Portrait is not writ large in my vocabulary. The human figure, clothed or unclothed, has always been of enormous interest to me but I don't regard myself as a portrait-painter. This, quite naturally, puts some people off. My paintings are situational and environmental – they are about what people are, what they do and where they do it. I have to know what they think about before I study what they look like.'

Born in 1913, Leonard Rosoman studied at the King Edward VII School of Art, Durham University, the Royal Academy Schools and the Central School of Art and Crafts in London. From 1943 to 1945 he was official war artist to the Admiralty. For much of his career he has taught at art schools in London and has given instruction in mural painting at Edinburgh College of Art. He was elected Associate of the Royal Academy (ARA) in 1960 and full Royal Academician (RA) in 1969. He was awarded the OBE in 1981.

Jack Smith b.1928

Jack Smith was born in 1928 in Sheffield, the heart of the industrial north Midlands. He attended Sheffield School of Art from 1944 to 1946, then joined the Royal Air Force at the age of eighteen. On leaving the RAF he attended St Martin's School of Art, London from 1948 to 1950. In 1949 he began a series of highly acclaimed sea paintings based on his memories of the west Scottish coast where he was based whilst in the RAF. At the Royal College of Art, from 1950 to 1953, he began to paint pictures of kitchens and children: compositions based on interiors and domestic life which perhaps gave the name to the Kitchen Sink School of which he was a prominent member.

In the 1960s Smith made a decisive move away from his more sombre compositions towards paintings infused with light. Lyrical abstract works followed, together with 'written pictures' which have both hieroglyphic and musical content, an approach to painting akin to that of Mondrian and Kandinsky.

One of our major abstract artists, Jack Smith has exhibited regularly. He won the first prize at the *John Moore's Liverpool Exhibition* in 1957, had a retrospective exhibition at the Whitechapel Art Gallery in 1959 and a major exhibition at the Serpentine Gallery in London in 1978. He designed the costumes for the Ballet Rambert's *Carmen Arcadiae* in 1986. He now lives in Sussex in the south of England.

Ruskin Spear CBE RA b.1911

Ruskin Spear's work forms part of the strong caricature tradition that has consistently emerged in British portraiture since the time of Hogarth. His depictions of eminent public figures and anonymous, humble characters are treated as paintings rather than portraits, so that the sitter becomes part of a larger composition. He uses a painterly style to exaggerate what he sees before him, heightening the traits that convey a sense of the sitter's character. His paintings are predominantly townscapes, chiefly of Hammersmith and other parts of west London, where he has spent most of his life.

Ruskin Spear was born in 1911 in Hammersmith, west London. He received a scholarship in 1926 to study at Hammersmith School of Art, and another in 1930 for the Royal College of Art, London. His early work was influenced by Sickert, and later on also by the Camden Town Group. From 1935 he taught at several art schools in London, including St Martin's School of Art. He was exempted from military service during World War II because of a childhood polio attack and supported himself by playing the piano in London dance bands and by producing fashion drawings for *Vogue* magazine. He was also commissioned by the War Artists Advisory Committee to paint pictures of the home front. He was elected Associate of the Royal Academy (ARA) in 1944, and Royal Academician (RA) in 1954. In 1948 he started teaching at the Royal College of Art, where his apparently light-hearted attitude, which belied an underlying deep sense of caring, was extremely influential on the young generation of Pop artists studying there in the 1950s. In 1949 Spear was elected President of the London Group. He was awarded the CBE in 1979. He currently lives and works in London.

George Newson

Sir Stanley Spencer Kt. CBE RA
1891-1959

Stanley Spencer was born in Cookham-on-Thames in Berkshire, a village that he loved and returned to time and again. Cookham has featured greatly in his work: Spencer throughout his career treated village life and the landscape of the countryside as vehicles for wider themes of religion and the union of the spirit and the body.

Early influences on Stanley Spencer were the Italian artists of the early Renaissance, particularly Giotto and Fra Angelico, and the Pre-Raphaelite painters. While they share a common subject matter, Spencer, like the Italians, set his religious scenes in his own time and place.

From 1902 to 1912 Spencer studied at the Slade School of Fine Art under Tonks; he was awarded a scholarship in 1910 and further prizes in 1912. During World War I he served in the Royal Army Medical Corps and was commissioned to paint an official war picture before his return from Macedonia where he was posted from 1916 to 1918. In World War II he was commissioned to paint pictures of shipyards by the War Artists Advisory Committee and the subjects he found at Lithgow's Yard, Port of Glasgow form a fine body of work undertaken between 1940 and 1946.

Always an independent artist, Spencer has, however, been grouped loosely with English Post-Impressionism. His original and often humorous vision and narrative powers set him apart from many of his contemporaries.

Spencer was elected Associate of the Royal Academy (ARA) in 1932; three years later he resigned from the Academy. After rejoining in 1950 he was elected Royal Academician (RA) and, that same year, was awarded the CBE. He received a knighthood in 1959, the year of his death.

Self-Portrait, before 1954, Williamson Art Gallery and Museum

Graham Sutherland OM 1903 – 80

Graham Sutherland, often regarded as one of the greatest twentieth-century British artists, is acclaimed for his portraiture and paintings of nature and religious subjects. Early small etchings featuring idyllic scenes of rural England were influenced by Samuel Palmer; these gave way to oil paintings during the mid-1930s, partly through the impact of the Pembrokeshire landscape on his work. Studies from nature in gouache – roots, branches, rocks – were squared up for oil paintings made in his studio, which became increasingly bold, stylized and densely coloured. The metamorphic nature of his images led to his inclusion in the International Surrealist Exhibition held in London in 1936. From the 1950s he painted numerous portraits of friends and distinguished personages. He became a Roman Catholic in 1926 and his religious images include a vast tapestry, *Christ in Glory in the Tetramorph*, designed for Coventry Cathedral between 1953 and 1961.

Graham Sutherland was born in London in 1903. His father was a lawyer and civil servant, and Sutherland grew up in Sutton, in Surrey. He studied at Goldsmiths' College of Art in London from 1921 to 1926, specializing in etching, and he taught part-time at Chelsea School of Art, London from 1927 to 1929. He worked as an official war artist from 1940 to 1945, documenting air-raid devastation, particularly during the Blitz in London. From 1947 onwards he made yearly visits to the South of France, the light there leading him to use brighter colours. In 1960 he was awarded the Order of Merit (OM). Sutherland's work is in numerous national collections, and in 1976 the Graham Sutherland Gallery at Picton Castle, Dyfed, in Wales was inaugurated.

David Tindle RA b.1932

Peter Wedgewood, Royal Academy Magazine

In the Romantic tradition of Samuel Palmer, but without his sometimes strident colour range, Tindle continues a thread in British painting that has not been followed by many of his contemporaries. The quality of light in his egg-tempera compositions is soft and pervasive, evoking an atmosphere of quiet that is at the same time slightly on edge. There is a feeling in the paintings that suggests undercurrents of unease, events that do not meet the eye. His still-life paintings, objects that are minutely observed, engage the spirit found in Morandi's work: simple things given grandeur through their disposition in space. His painting technique is painstaking, and the domestic interiors, landscapes, portraits and still-life compositions that result from applying layer upon layer of translucent colour, convey a subtle beauty that is timeless.

David Tindle was born in Huddersfield in 1932. He studied at Coventry School of Art from 1945 to 1947. He has taught throughout most of his career, variously at Hornsey College of Art, Byam Shaw College and the Royal College of Art, where he was elected Fellow in 1981. His last teaching position was that of Ruskin Master of Drawing at Oxford University between 1986 and 1987. He was elected Associate of the Royal Academy (ARA) in 1973 and Royal Academician (RA) in 1979.

Euan Uglow b.1932

Euan Uglow gives particular attention in painting to the size and proportion of the canvas and the precise, measured relationships between both subject and canvas, down to smaller areas of carefully defined tone and colour. The process of drawing is not concealed, exploratory lines and paintmarks remain, evincing a quality of openness which is found in the tradition of William Coldstream and, to a lesser extent, Patrick George.

The space between objects in a composition is as important as the shape of the objects themselves. Uglow's subjects are traditional: figures, portraits of friends, still lifes and landscapes. He brings to these a particular way of looking which extends our perception. Some works incorporate a reference to time and space. A model can move, a flower wilt, a piece of fruit decay: Uglow has sought in some of his canvases to record and analyse these physical changes through time.

Euan Uglow was born in London in 1932. From 1948 to 1951 he studied at Camberwell School of Art and Crafts and from 1951 to 1954 at the Slade School of Fine Art. He has taught at the Slade since 1961.

Peter Unsworth b.1937

Peter Unsworth works in oil, producing images which often have a photographic quality, frequently depicting figures frozen in mid action. He uses light tones to create soft, slightly unfocused images, peopled by shadowy, un-defined figures. The atmosphere in the works is often one of tension or expectation, and the stage-like quality of his paintings is echoed in the work commissioned from him by the Royal Ballet Company, for whom he designed the sets and costumes of three ballets.

Peter Unsworth was born in 1937 in County Durham in the north-east of England. He studied at Middlesborough School of Art, and at St Martin's School of Art in London. He has lived and painted in Greece and Spain, and currently divides his time between London and Ibiza.

Michael Upton b.1938

courtesy Anne Berthoud Gallery Ltd

Michael Upton's work has retained since the beginning a concern for the visual expression of time, continuity and change: change as affected by time and the way objects relate when their disposition in space is altered. He has expressed these ideas through photography and performance and now painting. The tonal range of his work is consciously limited, as is his use of colour. His politics are immediately evident in some works, together with social commentary: his working-class upbringing in the British Midlands has shaped Upton's political stance. His ideas, however, can find expression in a wide range of subjects that may take in a simple still life, a keyboard, a bicycle or figures in an interior.

Upton was born in Birmingham in 1938. He studied initially at Birmingham College of Art from 1954 to 1958 and then, until 1962, at the Royal Academy Schools in London, where he now teaches. Michael Upton has exhibited widely in Britain and abroad since 1966, and his work is represented in many public and private collections.

Keith Vaughan CBE 1912-1977

Born in 1912 in Selsey Bill in Sussex, Keith Vaughan was considered one of the best figurative painters working in Britain in the post-war years. He did not attend art school but painted in his spare time whilst working for an advertising agency in London from 1931 to 1938. During the war he served in the army, and had his first exhibition of drawings, made during the war, at the Lefevre Gallery, London in 1944.

The themes in his paintings remained constant throughout his career: the male nude in landscape, and pure landscape paintings. He taught for some years at both the Central School of Art and the Slade School of Fine Art in London. An extensive traveller, Vaughan visited Europe frequently and went also to the United States, Mexico and North Africa. His numerous exhibitions include retrospectives at the Whitechapel Art Gallery in 1962, the Mappin Art Gallery, Sheffield in 1969 and the University of York in 1970.

In 1956 he was awarded the CBE; in 1964 he received an Honorary Fellowship from the Royal College of Art. Keith Vaughan died in 1977.

Carel Weight CBE RA b.1908

Carel Weight says of himself: 'I am a humanist painter. But what interests me most about the human situation – or perhaps predicament would be a better word – is the ever present immanence of danger and disaster, of the sudden, unexpected, often terrible happening.'

Many of Carel Weight's urban scenes are set in south London where he lives and works, and are addressed to the people portrayed in them; shying away from art galleries and an art elite, Weight often prefers to sell his work directly to the public. Despite the predominance of typically English themes in his paintings, the strongest influences on his work have been German: he admires Breughel, Bosch and particularly Edvard Munch. Perhaps because of this his work is highly expressionistic, through the use of form and also colour, which plays an integral part in the design. Some of his paintings have religious themes and in 1963 he painted a mural in Manchester Cathedral depicting *Christ and the people*.

Carel Weight was born in 1908 in Paddington, London. He came from an affluent background but was sent to live with a working-class couple during the week, and so grew up in the poorer, rougher parts of Chelsea. In 1926 he attended Hammersmith School of Art and then studied part-time at Goldsmiths' College from 1929 to 1932. He taught painting there and in other London art schools until World War II, when he joined the forces. From 1945 to 1946 he was an official war artist, working in Italy, Greece and Austria. He joined the staff of the Royal College of Art, London in 1947, becoming Professor of Painting there in 1957. He was elected an Associate of the Royal Academy (ARA) in 1955, and full Royal Academician (RA) in 1965. He was a Trustee of the Academy from 1975 to 1984 and was awarded the CBE in 1961.

Laetitia Yhap b.1941

For some time after training at Camberwell School of Art and Crafts in London (from 1958 to 1962) Laetitia Yhap painted in an abstract manner, producing works in which the human figure was absent. However, at the end of the 1970s the influence of humanist themes in the work of artists such as Carpaccio, Donatello, Bosch, Breughel, Millet and Degas asserted itself in her paintings when she introduced a new, thematic content into her work: the everyday life of fishermen on the fishing beach at Hastings on the south-east coast of England. She constructs the boards for her paintings herself, creating shapes which deliberately distort geometrical forms and which heighten the restricted sense of space in the compositions. The beach scenes always look out to the sea, and the horizon is constantly evaded, drawing the spectator closer in to the scene. A wide range of almost unmixed oil colours are used in the paintings, and material elements evoking the fisherman's world, such as sand and rope, are often included in the works.

Laetitia Yhap was born in the coastal town of St Albans in 1941, and received a Leverhulme Research Award to travel in Italy in 1962-63 after finishing her first degree. She attended the Slade School of Fine Art from 1963 to 1965 and has exhibited widely in Britain since that time. She lives and works in Hastings.

Bibliography

Exhibition catalogues

1964   *Modern British Paintings, Drawings and Sculpture*
vols I and II, Tate Gallery, London
Mary Chamot, Denis Farr and Martin Butler

1976   *Arte inglese oggi 1960 – 76* (English art today)
Palazzo Reale Milan, The British Council and the Comune di Milano
Norbert Lynton, David Thompson, Richard Cork, Ted Little and David Curtis

1976   *The Human Clay*
Arts Council of Great Britain
selected by R B Kitaj

1977   *British Painting 1952 – 1977*
Royal Academy of Arts, London
selected by Frederick Gore RA

1984   *The British Art Show: old allegiances and new directions 1979 – 1984*
Arts Council of Great Britain, Orbis

1984   *The Hard-Won Image : traditional method and subject in recent British art*
Tate Galley, London
with text by Richard Morphet

1984   *The Proper Study : contemporary figurative painting from Britain*
Lalit Kala Akademi Delhi, Jehangir Museum of Art Bombay, The British Council
essays on artists by William Feaver, Catherine Lampert, Marco Livingstone, Paul Overy, David Sylvester

1985   *Human Interest : fifty years of British art about people*
Cornerhouse Gallery, Manchester
selected by Norbert Lynton

1987   *British Art in the Twentieth Century : the modern movement*
Royal Academy of Arts, London and Prestel-Verlag, Munich
edited by Susan Compton

1987   *A Paradise Lost : the neo-Romantic imagination in Britain*
Barbican Centre Gallery, Lund Humphries
with text by David Mellor

1987   *A School of London : six figurative painters*
The British Council
with essay by Michael Peppiatt

1987   *The Vigorous Imagination : new Scottish art*
Scottish National Gallery of Modern Art, Edinburgh

1988   *Exhibition Road : painters at the Royal College of Art*
The Royal College of Art, London in association with Phaidon and Christie's
edited by Paul Huxley

1988   *The New British Painting*
The Contemporary Arts Center, Cincinnati
Edward Lucie Smith, Carolyn Cohen and Judith Higgins

1989   *The Last Romantics : the Romantic tradition in British art, Burne Jones to Stanley Spencer*
Barbican Art Gallery, Lund Humphries

1989   *Scottish Art Since 1900*
Scottish National Gallery of Modern Art

Further reading

Hicks, Alistair *The School of London : the resurgence of contemporary painting* Phaidon Press, Oxford 1989

Kelly, Sean and Edward Lucie Smith *The Self-Portrait: a modern view* Sarema Press 1987

Laughton, Bruce *The Euston Road School* Scolar Press 1986

Lippard, Lucy *Pop Art* Thames and Hudson, London 1966

Livingstone, Marco ed. *British Figurative Painters* vols I and II Art Random, Kyoto 1989

Lynton, Norbert *The Story of Modern Art* Phaidon Press, Oxford 1980 rev. 1989

Rothenstein, John *British Art Since 1900 : an anthology* Phaidon Press, London 1962

Rothenstein, John *Modern English Painters* 3 vols MacDonald, London 1952 – 74, rev. 1984

Shone, Richard *A Century of Change : British painting since 1900* Oxford 1977

Spalding, Frances *British Art Since 1900* Thames and Hudson, London 1986

Yorke, Malcolm *The Spirit of Place : nine neo-Romantic artists and their times* Constable, London 1988

Index of artists

Catalogue numbers: italics
Page numbers: roman

Index of lenders

Catalogue numbers: italics
Page numbers: roman